The All-Volunteer Force

The All-Volunteer Force
A Study of Ideology in the Military

by
Jerald G. Bachman
John D. Blair
David R. Segal

Ann Arbor   **The University of Michigan Press**

Copyright © by The University of Michigan 1977
All rights reserved
Published in the United States of America by
The University of Michigan Press and simultaneously
in Rexdale, Canada, by John Wiley & Sons Canada, Limited
Manufactured in the United States of America

Library of Congress Cataloging in Publication Data

Bachman, Jerald G.
  The all-volunteer force.

  Bibliography: p.
  Includes index.
  1. Sociology, Military.   2.   United States—Armed
forces. 3.   Soldiers—United States.   I.   Blair, John
David, 1944–   joint author.   II.   Segal, David R.,
joint author.   III.   Title.
U21.5.B3   1977   301.5'93'0973   77-5631
ISBN 0-472-08095-4

Preface

What kinds of individuals will staff an all-volunteer military in the United States during the 1970s and beyond? That question has been a major focus for a series of policy-relevant research studies begun by the Institute for Social Research in 1968 and extending through 1976. The present publication draws from a number of these studies; in particular, it presents the results of a three-year exploration of perceptions and preferences about the military using data from large-scale surveys of soldiers, sailors, and civilians.

We view this study as an instance of policy-relevant research because we consider the staffing and the ideological makeup of the all-volunteer armed forces to be important national policy issues, and because we feel that the kinds of data we present can contribute to policy analyses and decisions. Our own viewpoints about the military have no doubt influenced our choice of research issues. However, we have tried to be objective in our analyses and have reported our findings extensively in the text and appendices so that readers with other points of view can examine the evidence in considerable detail.

Let us state at the outset our opinions about the all-volunteer army. We prefer that the armed forces be fundamentally responsive to civilian leadership, that they be well integrated with the larger civilian society, and that they be staffed by a broadly representative cross section of individuals reflecting a rich diversity of ideological perspectives. In other words, we seek to avoid what has been termed a "separate military ethos." This point of view is a value judgment, not something that can be demonstrated by survey research findings. As a matter of fact, our results suggest that issues of military staffing and ideology did not (as of 1973) worry the average citizen very much. But for those of us who do feel some concern about such matters, our findings suggest some of the impacts that all-volunteer conditions may have upon ideology within the military.

Stated briefly, our research indicates that if present (early 1977) practices for recruiting and retaining military personnel are continued, there is likely to be a gradual trend toward a more career-oriented military and a corresponding tendency toward a narrower "promilitary ideology" within the services. Our findings also suggest some steps which can be taken to arrest and even reverse the trend. But the decision as to whether the trend *should* be reversed cannot be derived from research alone. It is a policy judgment that must be made by the nation's leaders. Our hope is that the research reported here can make some contribution to that decision-making process.

Our involvement in this particular area of research developed along separate and different paths. Jerald Bachman's interest grew out of a longitudinal study of youth. As an outgrowth of that project, he and Jerome Johnston began (in 1968) extensive analyses of young men's views and personal decisions about the military. That led to a three-year collaboration with David Bowers, funded first by the U.S. Office of Naval Research (1972–74) and then by the U.S. Army Research Institute (1974–75), which generated most of the data reported here.

While Bachman was studying aspects of the military from a detached vantage point in the Institute for Social Research, John Blair was studying the military as a participant-observer—his graduate studies in sociology had been interrupted by a tour of duty as an Army officer (1968–71), which included service in Vietnam. The experience prompted an interest in military sociology. It eventually led to a full-time analysis and writing collaboration with Bachman, before Blair joined the faculty of the University of Maryland in 1975.

David Segal's interest in military sociology developed when he was a graduate student at the University of Chicago. In 1966 he joined the sociology faculty at the University of Michigan, where he later had occasion to work with Blair. From 1973 to early 1976 he directed the Social Processes Technical Area of the U.S. Army Research Institute. During this period our Army survey was conducted under the sponsorship of his division. His collaboration on this book took place later in 1976 after he joined the faculty of the University of Maryland.

In preparing this publication, our contributions have been different and our involvement has varied, but we share an equal responsibility for the final product. We have drawn from a number of our earlier works, some authored separately and others authored jointly. These include "The Public View of the Military" and "Citizen Force or Career Force" by Jerald Bachman and John Blair, originally published in *The Social Psychology of Military Service*, edited by Nancy L. Goldman and David R. Segal. An abridged version of the "Citizen Force or Career Force" paper was also published in *Armed Forces and Society, Volume 2*. "Public Confidence in the U.S. Military" by Segal and Blair was published in *Armed Forces and Society, Volume 3*. We are grateful to Sage Publications and the Inter-University Seminar on Armed Forces and Society for permission to reprint portions of this material.

The first, and in some respects the most detailed, reporting of our survey findings occurred in two technical reports to the Office of Naval Research and one technical report to the Army Research Institute: "Values, Preferences and Perceptions Concerning Military Service, Part I and Part II," by Bachman; and "Soldiers, Sailors and Civilians," by Bachman and Blair. All are available from the National Technical Information Service.

A number of our colleagues contributed to this work by reviewing portions of the text, providing advice on data analysis, collaborating in research and instrument design, and in other ways. In particular, we are very grateful to David G. Bowers, Angus Campbell, John H. Faris, Morris Janowitz, M. Kent Jennings, Jerome Johnston, Lloyd D. Johnston, Scott McNall, Michael K. Moch, Charles C. Moskos, Jr., and Patrick M. O'Malley.

An effort of this sort also involves the participation of literally hundreds of interviewers and other research staff members. We cannot acknowledge all of the contributions individually, but we do want to express our thanks to the Sampling, Field and Coding Sections of the Survey Research Center, which contributed to the survey of civilians, and to staff members in the Center for Research on the Utilization of Scientific Knowledge, and also to military staff members who together made possible the data collections from Army and Navy personnel.

The data computations for this report employed the OSIRIS computer software system, which was jointly developed by the component centers of the Institute for Social Research using funds from the National Science Foundation, the Inter-University Consortium for Political Research, and other sources. Much of the actual analysis work was ably carried out by Donna Ando and by Ellen Berger. We would also like to acknowledge Kevin Urick and Judy Redmond for the typing and the manuscript preparation, and Barbara Ann Lynch who prepared the bibliography.

A final word of thanks is reserved for the thousands of soldiers, sailors, and civilians who participated in our surveys. We hope we have reflected their viewpoints faithfully.

Some of the research reported here was funded by the Office of Naval Research, Organizational Effectiveness Research Programs, under contract no. N00014–67–A–0181–0048, and by the U.S. Army Research Institute for the Behavioral and Social Sciences, under grant DAHC19–74–G–0017. The views expressed herein are those of the authors and do not represent institutional positions of the Department of the Navy or the Department of the Army.

Contents

Introduction

Who should serve in the armed forces of the United States? What should be the relationship between the armed forces and civilian society? These fundamental questions were of vital interest to the nation's founders and first leaders. They continued to be of concern throughout the following two centuries. Now, as the nation begins its third century, technology has produced truly awesome capabilities for mass destruction; and questions about who should staff and who should control the military remain as vital as ever.

This book deals with the all-volunteer armed forces in the United States. While the fundamental questions are not new, the social context and our research methods are. We have employed the methods of survey research to examine the ways in which both civilians and military personnel view the armed forces in the 1970s. We do not suggest that survey data can or should provide direct answers to fundamental questions of national military policy. Our aims are much more modest. We believe that the findings presented here can provide some new perspectives on present military personnel practices and the ways in which these practices, perhaps quite inadvertantly, may be shaping the nature of military staffing and civil-military relations.

Research Methods: Samples and Measures

Our research strategy is to examine and to compare the views of military men and civilians. Our findings are based on survey questionnaires—identical except for certain personal background measures—administered to three samples: (1) a representative national cross section of the civilian population surveyed in early 1973; (2) a sample of Navy personnel in late 1972 and early 1973, stratified so as to be representative of major Navy entities (ships and shore stations); and (3) a sample of Army personnel in late 1974 and early 1975, stratified to represent major Army entities. Thus, we are able to represent soldiers, sailors, and civilians, all responding to the same questions about the U.S. military and its mission. (The samples are described in greater detail in Appendix A.)

The numbers of women in the Army and Navy samples are very small and somewhat unevenly distributed throughout the analysis groupings. That means that in reality our samples permit us to represent military men, not military men and women. Accordingly, we have taken what seems the simplest and least confusing approach, and have limited analyses of Army and Navy data in the present report to male respondents. Nevertheless, we believe that our findings based on military men in 1972–75, and the issues that we discuss in connection with these findings, are applicable to women as well as men in the armed forces during the 1970s.

The questionnaires administered to all three samples included a series of items dealing with values, preferences, and perceptions about the military. The questions were designed in such a way that they could be answered by both civilians and servicemen. It seems likely, of course, that the Army and Navy respondents answered some of these items with particular reference to their own experience in the service, whereas many civilians answered with a more general frame of reference. Nevertheless, we think that the questions are in many respects quite comparable for both service personnel and civilians. The relevant questionnaire segment is reproduced in Appendix E.

Overview

As we noted earlier, our survey data deal with fundamental policy issues. Some of those issues are examined in chapter 1. The chapter begins with a review of recent history as it has affected the military and its personnel policies, particularly the shift to an all-volunteer force. The chapter then summarizes two alternative models of civilian control over the military, and concludes with a discussion of whether those who serve in the all-volunteer military are likely to be demographically and ideologically similar to their civilian counterparts.

Chapter 2 reviews the findings from a number of different surveys which included questions about the military and military leadership. The results, covering the period from 1964 through 1976, provide useful perspectives on the ways in which public opinion concerning the military has changed in some respects and remained nearly constant in other respects.

Chapter 3 continues the emphasis on civilian views about the military, but the attention shifts to an in-depth study of our sample of civilians surveyed in early 1973. This chapter introduces sixteen dimensions of military views which are used throughout the next several chapters; it also presents data suggesting that it is sometimes useful to think in terms of a single continuum of attitudes ranging from promilitary to antimilitary. The chapter describes the civilian population as a whole, and then explores important differences linked to age, education, and prior military experience.

Chapter 4 examines the views of Navy and Army men along the dimensions introduced in chapter 3. Distinctions are drawn between officers and enlisted men, and between those with career interests in the military and those planning to leave after their current tour of duty. Differences and similarities between the Navy and Army data are examined with special attention given to the two-year interval between the data collections. Two alternative explanations—attitude change versus self-selection—are explored as possible bases for the differences between career and noncareer servicemen.

Chapter 5 presents a comparison between civilian and military views. The key military groups examined in chapter 4 are compared with civilians matched in terms of age and education. These comparisons provide convincing evidence for military distinctiveness in beliefs, but only in the case of career men. The noncareerists are in most respects quite similar to their civilian counterparts.

Chapter 6 extends the comparison of civilians and military men by taking a detailed look at views about the influence of military leaders versus civilian leaders in matters affecting national security policy. The findings again show substantial differences between the views of career military men and civilians, and raise concerns about civil-military relations.

Chapter 7 presents an integration and interpretation of the findings, including an attempt to spell out policy implications. Special attention is given to military staffing under all-volunteer conditions in ways that could preserve a substantial proportion of citizen-soldiers, those who view a tour of military service as a relatively temporary departure from civilian life.

1
Who Serves in the Armed Forces? Implications for Civil-Military Relations

Who should serve in the armed forces of the United States? This very broad question gives rise to a number of other questions. Some are quantitative and straightforward. How many people are needed? How high a pay scale will be necessary to recruit and retain a sufficient number? What will it cost? Some questions are qualitative and more subtle. What levels of skill and ability are needed? How important is it for military personnel to be representative of the larger civilian society in terms of demographic characteristics, such as socioeconomic status and race? How important is it for them to be *ideologically* representative, i.e., that their views of the military and its mission be similar to the views held by civilians? What is the role of the citizen-soldier in the modern military?

The quantitative questions figured most prominently in the debate during the late sixties and early seventies over whether the United States could, and should, convert to an all-volunteer armed force. The quantitative questions were answered, at least to some extent. The nation put an end to conscription and turned to a military which was staffed entirely with volunteers. The more subtle and qualitative questions were also raised in the debate, but the answers were less clear.

This book is concerned with those questions regarding *what kinds* of individuals now serve in the armed forces, what views they hold about the military and military decision making, and how these views might affect civil-military relations. In this chapter we first try to gain some historical perspective on the movement away from a mass military force and toward an all-volunteer force. Next, we consider two different models of civilian control over the military. Then we discuss the issue of representativeness—the match between military personnel and civilians—and how that match may be affected by the conversion to the all-volunteer force.

The Decline of the Mass Military Force

In the 1970s, a new era of military organization and of civil-military relations emerged in the United States. For the previous two decades the domestic policies of the nation had included two "wars": one against racism, manifested most dramatically by the civil rights movement, and the other against poverty, a high priority on the federal government agenda. In the international arena, the United States was finally extricating itself from a long, painful, and ultimately unsuccessful military conflict in Southeast Asia. As that war dragged on, its popular support plummeted. We shall see in the following chapter that as support for the Vietnam conflict waned, public confidence in the federal government, which was responsible for the formulation of military policy, dropped as well.

Unlike previous major American military conflicts of the twentieth century—two world wars and the Korean Police Action—the Vietnam War was fought without mass mobilization of military reserve capabilities. The decision to wage a war in Southeast Asia without resorting to the use of the reserves increased the dependence of the military establishment upon its conscription system, the Selective Service, to supply the personnel resources needed to field a combat force. It also reflected a denial of an important component of the form of military organization on which America had depended during the first half of the century—the mass army.

The mass military force, based upon conscription of some fraction of the citizenry, had itself represented a unique era in military organization. Prior to the American and French revolutions, the rights to bear arms in defense of the country, and particularly to serve as a military officer, were generally restricted to a hereditary nobility in Western society. In the course of these two revolutions, however, the definition of the citizenry, that is, those segments of the population which could legitimately claim a role in the political process, was expanded. Moreover, participation in armed conflict became an integral aspect of the normative definition of citizenship (Janowitz, 1975, pp. 70–88).

The arming of the citizenry and the broadening of the social basis of recruitment to the officer corps provided avenues to citizenship rights. The career military nucleus was supplemented by two classes of citizen-soldier; the conscript (and those volunteers who enlisted in the armed forces to avoid being drafted), and the reservist (many of whom joined the reserves to avoid being drafted). The conscript was regarded by Engels as more important than the general franchise in the establishment of political democracy, and the reservist is seen by Morris Janowitz as a vehicle for the maintenance of civilian control over military professionals. The long-term rise of the mass army in the world system had in common with the American civil rights movement and the War against Poverty the effect of reducing certain forms of inequality in society and broadening the extent of citizen participation in the polity. They were all tied in some way to the citizenship revolution (Bendix, 1964), and they all had an impact on the relationship between the role of citizen and that of soldier.

The mass army reached the height of its importance in the Western world during the first half of the twentieth century. The armies of that era were mass in terms of size, with the U.S. Army numbering almost 6 million during World War II. They were mass in terms of having low levels of organizational differentiation, with the infantry serving as the prototypical model of the soldier. And they were mass in terms of the mobilization of people and resources drawn from the civilian sector (Van Doorn, 1975, pp. 53–56). The mass army represented the fusion of the military institution and the civilian sector of industrial society.

The mass armed force is itself on the wane today. The technological basis for the decline of the mass force appeared in World War II with the advent of nuclear weapons. The new technology of warfare had four major impacts on the military institution. First, while not making infantry warfare obsolete by any means, it made control of the air a higher priority, and indeed a necessary condition for control over the ground. The shift required greater skill differentiation and greater technological sophistication within the military, thus bringing the distribution of skills within the military more closely into line with that which existed in the civilian society.

Second, this change in technology affected the number of people required for military operations. As technology was substituted for infantry, the size of the force decreased. And within the force, the proportion needed for traditional combat activities decreased as the technical specialties expanded. Thus, fewer people were to bear arms in defense of the state, at least in the traditional sense, and it became increasingly difficult to identify what about the military was truly unique (Biderman, 1967).

Third, new military technologies made it possible to deliver devastating firepower upon dense centers of civilian population, thus putting the civilian, as well as the front-line soldier, in danger of war-related injury. This socialization of danger further reduced the differential between the military and the civilian.

Fourth, the blurring of the boundary between military and civilian institutions precipitated a potential problem of legitimacy for the military. Not very long ago the mission of defending the country meant that people whose day-to-day activities were considerably different from those of the civilian labor force could, through their activities, protect civilian concentrations at great risk to themselves. Under those conditions a normative system emerged that defined the military institution as useful and legitimate. Now, however, the activities of military personnel are more similar to the activities of civilians, and civilians are not necessarily insulated from the danger of warfare. As a result, the legitimacy of the armed forces and the degree to which they serve the needs of society have become subject to question.

The decline of the mass army plus the widespread questioning of the legitimacy of the military institution and the Vietnam War served to confound the relationship between the military and the citizen-soldier. The decision not to utilize military reserves to fill out and to provide replacements for regular combat units kept one model of citizen-soldier—the reservist—out of the Vietnam War. But this was done at the expense of another kind of citizen-soldier, the military conscript, and it may well have overburdened the Selective Service System. The popularity of military conscription varied widely throughout American history, and in the mid-1960s it was clear that support for Vietnam-era conscription was declining.

The Shift to an All-Volunteer Armed Force

The military draft, never very popular during the post-World War II era, came under increasing criticism in the 1960s. By 1966 there were widespread student demonstrations against the draft and its inequities. On July 1 of that year, President Johnson appointed a national advisory commission on Selective Service (the Marshall commission). This commission was charged to "consider the past, present, and prospective functioning of selective service and other systems of national service in the light of the following factors: fairness to all citizens; military manpower requirements; the objective of minimizing uncertainty and interference with individual careers and education; social, economic, and employment conditions and goals; budgetary and administrative consideration . . . " (Tax, 1967, p. 466).

Shortly before the Marshall commission was appointed, the University of Chicago began plans for a national conference on the draft. The Chicago conference took place in December, 1966, under the chairmanship of Sol Tax. It brought together a wide range of participants including social scientists, legislators, military leaders, and also the executive director of the Marshall commission, Bradley H. Patterson, Jr. Mr. Patterson attended the conference for the explicit purpose of ensuring that the Marshall commission had full benefit of the ideas and recommendations generated at the Chicago conference. A number of viewpoints were expressed in prepared papers and in careful discussions. Indeed, the majority of ideas which have been the focus of discussion in more recent years were represented at the 1966 Chicago conference. No genuine consensus emerged from the conference; nevertheless, there did appear to be a considerable depth and range of support for an all-volunteer armed force as an alternative to the draft.[1]

In March of 1967 President Johnson proposed that Congress enact a four-year extension of the authority to induct men into the armed forces. His proposal also included a number of reforms in the Selective Service System intended to make the system more fair and less disruptive to young men. The president's message to Congress stated a clear preference for a military based entirely on volunteers, but concluded that unfortunately this was not feasible for two reasons. First, the president felt that an all-volunteer

---

1. The products of the University of Chicago conference on the draft, both position papers and transcripts of the discussions, are contained in a volume edited by Tax (1967).

It should be noted that an all-volunteer force was not the only alternative which had been proposed to take the place of the draft system. Other possibilities included universal military training, or mandatory national service (which provide both military and nonmilitary alternatives for serving the national needs).

force could not be expanded quickly to meet a sudden challenge. Second, an all-volunteer force would probably be very expensive.

Support for an all-volunteer force continued to grow, however, and in 1969 President Nixon announced the appointment of an advisory commission on an all-volunteer armed force, chaired by former Secretary of Defense Thomas S. Gates, Jr. In 1970 the Gates commission submitted its report to the president. The following excerpt captures much of the substance and spirit of the report:

> ... However necessary conscription may have been in World War II, it has revealed many disadvantages in the past generation. It has been a costly, inequitable, and divisive procedure for recruiting men for the armed forces. It has imposed heavy burdens on a small minority of young men while easing slightly the tax burden on the rest of us. It has introduced needless uncertainty into the lives of all our young men. It has burdened draft boards with painful decisions about who shall be compelled to serve and who shall be deferred. It has weakened the political fabric of our society and impaired the delicate web of shared values that alone enables a free society to exist.
>
> These costs of conscription would have to be borne if they were a necessary price for defending our peace and security. They are intolerable when there is an alternative consistent with our basic national values. (United States President's Commission on an All-Volunteer Armed Force, 1970, pp. 9–10)

The Gates commission proposed an all-volunteer force as the alternative, and recommended three basic steps necessary to attain it: higher military salaries, improved conditions of service and recruiting, and the establishment of a standby draft system. The commission also dealt specifically with many of the questions and objections raised in opposition to an all-volunteer force.

President Nixon accepted the major conclusions of the Gates commission. In a message to Congress in April, 1970, he stated his objective to reduce draft calls to zero, and outlined a series of pay increases and other steps designed to reach that objective. He addressed the Congress again in January, 1971, where he proposed further steps to move toward the goal of an all-volunteer force, but also requested an extension of the draft. The president requested only a two-year extension of induction authority, and coupled this request with proposals for reform of the draft. The question of extending the draft for even two years was debated vigorously, but eventually the extension was enacted. Later in 1971, Congress voted substantial increases in military pay. While these increases were not as high as the Gates commission recommendation, they did almost double the average monthly pay for new recruits.

One of the reasons for declining support of the draft, of course, was declining support for the Vietnam War itself. A second reason was that the military draft was perceived to discriminate against precisely those individuals whose lot the civil rights movement and the War against Poverty sought to improve—blacks and poor people. It was widely felt that there were two economic costs borne by those who were drafted to serve. In the short run, draftees were paid considerably less than they would have earned in industry. In the long run, it was believed that they would experience a decrease in lifetime earnings by being in the military at a time when their age peers were embarking on civilian careers (e.g., Miller and Tollison, 1971).

Research on the social representativeness of the conscription-era armed force has produced somewhat mixed findings. Davis and Dolbeare (1968) found the poor to be overrepresented among draftees, a fact that is especially impressive given that those with low incomes were also much more likely than those with high incomes to be found mentally, morally, or physically unfit for service. In short, they argued that men with low incomes who were qualified for service were far more likely to be drafted than men with high incomes who had similar qualifications. They also found blacks to be overrepresented among draftees, but only as a function of their representation in low-income strata. Blacks were not drafted in any greater proportions than whites of the same economic strata. In other words, blacks drafted through the Selective Service System were victims of economic, not racial, discrimination. More recent research, while it does not confront the issue of stratification by income, suggests a different pattern of representation during conscription. Father's occupation, an alternate indication of social background, was *not* found to be related to whether one was drafted. Father's education, however, was *positively* related to the likelihood of being drafted since men from more literate backgrounds would be more likely to pass the armed forces' mental screening tests (Fligstein, 1976). In this analysis, blacks were shown to be discriminated against, i.e., underselected, by the draft.

Empirical research has likewise not shown the existence of long-term economic costs presumed to have been borne by those who were drafted. Most research shows no significant impact of military service on postservice earnings (Cutright, 1974; Mason, 1970; Segal and Segal, 1976). Moreover, Browning et al. (1973) and Lopreato and Poston (1976) suggest that the military may provide a "bridging environment" for people of disadvantaged social backgrounds by preparing and certifying them for jobs in the civilian economy, thus enabling them to earn more than their peers who did not serve. This of course is not to deny that in the short run, recent veterans may experience difficulty in locating jobs in the civilian labor force.

During the conscription era it was also felt that if some segments of the population were overrepresented in the military as a result of being drafted, they would likewise be overrepresented among military casualties. And it seemed unfair to ask those segments of the population who reaped the least from society to sacrifice the most in time of war. Even in the face of a questionable relationship between position in the stratification system and likelihood of being drafted, individuals from lower socioeconomic backgrounds, once they were drafted, were more likely to be channeled into the ground combat forces than into branches requiring technical aptitudes. They were, therefore, also more likely to be wounded or killed than were persons of higher socioeconomic backgrounds (Badillo and Curry, 1976). Again, blacks were overrepresented in these strata, and through socioeconomic rather than racial discrimination were overrepresented among casualties.

During the Vietnam War, in contrast to previous American wars, education was inversely related to military service. Student deferments had a statistically significant effect on the draft. In an effort to make military conscription more equitable, the system of deferments that allowed people to escape the draft was revised, as was the method of selection for service. These steps were taken too late to save the Selective Service System. In 1967, eligibility for student deferments was reduced to age twenty-four or four years of study, whichever occurred first. In 1968, deferments for all graduate study except medicine and allied fields were ended. In 1969, there was a sharp reduction in draft calls, and in 1970, much of the discretionary power of local Selective Service boards was eliminated by the establishment of the draft lottery. This lottery assigned Selective Service registrants priorities for conscription on the basis of their birth dates. These changes increased the likelihood that males from higher socioeconomic backgrounds would be drafted, and may well have increased opposition to the draft among those whose risk of conscription had increased. In 1971, the Selective Service law expired but was extended for two years by Congress, although draft calls remained low. In January, 1973, six months earlier than required by Congress, Secretary of Defense Melvin Laird announced the end of peacetime conscription.

The end of conscription, an important component of the mass army, drastically altered the relationship between the roles of citizen and soldier. Where conscription had produced an armed force that was, by and large, representative of American society, it was feared during the debate on the all-volunteer force that such a force would indeed place the burden of defending the country disproportionately on the shoulders of the poor and the black (Marmion, 1971), and that there would be virtually no college-educated personnel in the enlisted ranks (Janowitz, 1973). In short, the volunteer force was subjected to the same criticisms as the conscription-era force had been. More importantly in terms of civil-military relations, the transition to an all-volunteer force was seen as narrowing the social base both for officer recruitment and for that remaining vestige of the mass army, the reserves (Janowitz, 1971).

Models of Civilian Control

Much of the scholarly debate on the maintenance of civilian control of the American military has focused on two models which Huntington (1957) refers to as "objective" versus "subjective" control. The objective model, which Huntington prefers, assumes an apolitical professional military relatively isolated from civilian institutions and responsible to a formal chain of command. That chain of command is controlled by civilian decision makers, some elected, such as the president in his role as commander in chief, and some appointed, such as the secretaries of defense and of the services, with checks and balances built into the system by the power of the Congress to declare war. In the objective system, as long as (a) the federal administration is responsive to the electorate, (b) the system of checks and balances between executive and legislative branches operates smoothly, and (c) the chain of command functions effectively, civilian control of the military can be maintained. Consequently, it should not matter whether the active-duty military force is representative of, or closely integrated with, the broader civilian society.

Janowitz (1960) proposes an alternative model which Huntington would regard as subjective control. Having learned from the study of complex organizations that informal organization is a better predictor of actual behavior than is the formal organization chart (see e.g., Blau, 1955), Janowitz proposes a military force integrated with its host society rather than isolated from it. This would ensure that civilian control can be achieved through political sensitivity rather than neutrality. Rather than placing complete trust in the president being responsive to the will of the people, the system of checks and balances operating smoothly, and the chain of command functioning effectively, Janowitz prefers that there also be informal processes which will ensure that civilian sensibilities are incorporated within the military. The informal processes of control preferred by Janowitz can operate through social networks that span the boundary between civilian and military institutions and bring military personnel into direct contact with the civilian community. Informal control can also occur through the presence in the military of personnel whose primary identities are as civilians rather than as military careerists. In the past these were the draftee and reservist citizen-soldiers.

But circumstances have changed, and it appears that the informal processes of control have been weakened. The Vietnam era brought about the end of peacetime conscription and the atrophy of the reserves. The density of informal social networks that span the civil-military boundary is relatively low (Segal, 1975). Janowitz (1975) has recently argued that with the end of military conscription (*a*) the military has come to emphasize distinctive values; (*b*) its linkages to civilian society have become attenuated and tied to limited segments of the social structure; (*c*) through changes in the recruitment base both the officer corps and the enlisted force are becoming less representative of society; and (*d*) such processes can create an "ideological caste" in the military and serve as a source of political cleavage.

We agree with Larson (1974) that Janowitz's model seems better suited to meeting the problems of American civil-military relations in the post-Vietnam era of an all-volunteer armed force than does Huntington's objective model. But in order for the Janowitz model to function, the armed forces must be broadly representative of American society.

Issue of Representativeness

To what extent are the armed forces representative? To what degree is the military staffed by people who are basically similar to most civilians? The representativeness of the armed forces must be considered on two different levels. On the one hand, we are interested in all military personnel and the extent to which they are representative of the larger civilian society. On the other hand, we must give special attention to career military personnel, particularly the career-oriented officer corps.

Most of the debate on the representativeness of the armed forces has focused on social background characteristics of military personnel. Kronenberg (1974, p. 323), for example, suggests that with the enlisted ranks being drawn from lower socioeconomic strata and officers from ROTC programs at nonelite campuses, "the U.S. armed forces will become increasingly less representative of the general population and perhaps prone to castelike inbreeding." Janowitz and Moskos (1974) raise the specter of an increasingly high concentration of black soldiers in the ground combat forces which would lead to increased racial tensions within the services, apprehension about the internal reliability of a force so composed, and the impact of disproportionately high black casuality rates in time of war. We do not deny either the overrepresentation of blacks in the all-volunteer force or the importance of these problems; however, our own view is that the paramount issue in American civil-military relations in the all-volunteer era is the ideological rather than the demographic representativeness of the armed forces.

It is worthwhile to note here the relationship between representativeness of the force and quality of the personnel. The all-volunteer force presently overrepresents the lower socioeconomic, educational, and skill strata (Segal and

Daina, 1975). Steps which might be taken to make the force more demographically and ideologically representative are also likely to increase literacy and skill levels.

Career Military Personnel

Under the mass army system, it was widely recognized that the professional military nucleus was at least somewhat more conservative than the civilian population at large (Janowitz, 1960), and perhaps considerably more so (Huntington, 1957). The draftees and reservists who served under and alongside the professional nucleus served both to represent civilian attitudes within the military and to provide structural linkages between the military and the civilian population. And while concern has periodically been voiced that the process of military training and socialization increases conservatism and authoritarianism (e.g., Christie, 1952), the bulk of the evidence does not support this proposition (Campbell and McCormack, 1957; Roghmann and Sodeur, 1972). Rather, the conservatism of career military personnel seems in the main due to self-selection, and secondarily due to the professionalization of the career military nucleus (Abrahamsson, 1972).

The issue of professionalism is itself problematic in the analysis of civil-military relations. Huntington sees the professionalization of the officer corps as supporting the norm of political neutrality of the military. There are three major problems with this formulation. First, the concept of a profession applies at best to a small proportion of the career force—the career-oriented officer corps. To the extent that military professionalism is a necessary component of civilian control, a large part of the military cadre is beyond its pale. Second, due to some structural changes in the Western nations, it is not clear whether the career officer corps indeed constitutes a profession, or whether it merely represents an occupational group (Abrams, 1965; Moskos, 1976). It is questionable whether the traits that have historically characterized medicine, law, and the clergy are typical of the modern military officer. Third, and perhaps most important, if indeed the career officer nucleus does constitute a profession, it is not clear, as Huntington assumes, that the professional ethic will assume political neutrality of the military. The medical and legal professions are without doubt active forces in modern politics. Abrahamsson (1972) has, in fact, argued that the process of professionalization will inevitably transform the military into a corporate interest group which, rather than subjecting itself to civilian control, will seek to increase its political autonomy and expand its political role. In Abrahamsson's view, internalization of norms restricting the political role of the military, which is a necessary component of Huntington's objective model, is unlikely to take place in the process of professionalization.

Whether or not the values and perceptions of military personnel in the all-volunteer force truly constitute a professional ideology, the central questions remain the same. Are career military personnel distinctly different from civilians in their views about the military and its mission? In particular, do the careerists see the proper role of the military as including subordination to civilian control? If we could be confident that the career force is not ideologically different from the civilian population, or if we could be sure that the ideology of the career force clearly and incontrovertibly assumes subordination of the military to civilian authority and that the control mechanisms assumed by Huntington really do operate effectively, then we would be less concerned about civil-military relations and the issue of representativeness. But, as we shall see in the following chapters, our survey data do not permit that degree of optimism about the career force. There do appear to be important ideological differences between career military men and civilians. One of these key differences concerns the amount of influence that military leaders ought to have.

It may be that during the conscription era civilian control was strengthened by an armed force which was at least somewhat representative of the civilian society, with citizen-soldiers playing a countervailing role against the career force. Now, under the current all-volunteer conditions, the tendency may be to recruit military personnel who are less fully representative of society in terms of social background and beliefs about the role of the military. Moreover, there is reason to assume that greater proportions of recruits will reenlist and will come to view the military as a career rather than as a temporary departure from their civilian status. To the extent that these several observations are accurate, we see a growing need to resurrect the role of the citizen-soldier within the current all-volunteer armed force.

In its projections for the future under all-volunteer conditions, the U.S. President's Commission on an All-Volunteer Force (1970, p. 133) had assumed that the composition of the all-volunteer force in terms of career orientation would not differ greatly from that found in the conscription era. Reenlistment data reported by the Department of the Army (1975) indicate that this assumption by the president's commission may have been in error. Reenlistment rates among first-term personnel in the Regular Army (i.e., with draftees excluded) rose from 18 percent in 1970 to 40 percent as of mid-1975. Among later term personnel the rise during that period was from 63 percent to 75 percent. For the total Regular Army (first term and later term combined) the reenlistment rate rose from 31 percent in 1970 to 54 percent by mid-1975. Since reenlistment rates clearly affect the overall proportion of reenlistees versus first-term enlistees, we conclude that the president's commission may have underestimated the relative size of the "career force" which might develop under all-volunteer conditions. And we view this larger career-force as potentially problematic.

The Changed Nature of "Military Employment"

One of the reasons for higher rates of reenlistment among first-term personnel may have to do with the changed pattern of compensation for military employment. Since the transition to an all-volunteer force, policy makers have increasingly acted as though military work roles were equivalent to civilian occupations. Indeed, the U.S. President's Commission on an All-Volunteer Armed Force (1970) recommended that military compensation be based on a "salary" system similar to that of civilian industry, that lateral hiring of trained personnel from the civilian labor force be increased, and that, in general, the all-volunteer services compete with industry for quality personnel as similar (although not identical) entities.

Prior to the transition to an all-volunteer force, military pay lagged behind civilian pay in the United States. Between 1951 and 1966, for example, military pay rose 60 percent. During the same period, General Schedule civil service pay, which is adjusted to increases in salary levels in private industry, rose more than 70 percent. Moreover, first-term military personnel received no pay increase in the 1951–64 period. During the transition to an all-volunteer force, however, efforts were made to make the military competitive with civilian employment in terms of pay. Between 1967 and 1975, Regular Military Compensation (RMC)—the sum of base pay, quarters and subsistence allowances, and tax advantage—increased 87 percent, while General Schedule civil service salaries increased 55 percent; and in 1971, a large pay increase was given to the first-term soldier. Pay for military personnel (RMC) is now roughly equivalent to that of civil service personnel at comparable grade levels. A 1974 survey of conditions of military service in the Western nations reported that while all these nations had their military pay structured "in relationship to civilian employment," only the United States, Canada, and the United Kingdom indicated that their service pay scales were comparable to civilian employment (Assembly of Western European Union, 1974).

In the years prior to the establishment of equivalency between RMC and General Schedule pay levels, the economic disadvantages of military service were, in part, offset by fringe benefits that came to be viewed as part of the compensation package in an implied contract (see chapter 8). These benefits included housing or housing allowances, health care for dependents, educational benefits, commissaries, and post exchanges. Among the latent functions of this pattern of compensation were: support of the military occupation as a calling rather than simply an occupation, maintenance of the military installation as a community, enhancement of the fraternal nature of military organization, legitimation of the military as a social institution, and incentive for the citizen to serve as a soldier and fulfill a right and responsibility of citizenship.

With the move toward equalizing military pay levels with civilian pay levels, and the attendant increases in direct personnel costs in the armed forces, there have been changes in the structure of benefits that differ from what have been regarded as the terms of the implied contract. There have been decreases in the availability of medical care to military dependents and retirees and cutbacks in allowances for travel and for shipment of household goods. Postgraduate education benefits for active military personnel have been cut back. Appropriated fund support for military commissaries has been under attack. And junior officers with good service records, who desired military careers, have been discharged from the service through reductions in force before they could become eligible for retirement benefits.

In sum, the conditions of working for the armed forces as a uniformed member of the service have increasingly come to resemble the employment conditions of a civilian occupation. Whether by design, intuition, or accident, the makers of military personnel policy have sought to compete with commerce and industry for citizen-workers by making military employment increasingly similar to civilian employment.

It seems to us that these developments are not likely to enlarge the number of citizen-soldiers, those individuals who expect to serve for a single tour of duty before returning to civilian life. Instead, military service may increasingly come to attract only a limited subset of the total work force, those who see military service as relatively more attractive

than the civilian work roles available to them. It seems likely
that a substantial proportion of such individuals will be interested in more than just a single term of service; the same
things which make the military attractive to them initially
are likely to make additional tours of duty more attractive.
Moreover, given that there are only a limited set of positions at higher levels on the military career ladder, these
larger numbers of individuals with career interests are likely
to experience a more competitive situation than heretofore
existed. That in turn may generate more pressures to conform and become "organization men" who avoid anything
which would jeopardize chances for advancement.

Conclusions and Implications

The last few decades have seen sweeping changes in the
nature of the U.S. military and its relationship with the
civilian society. The development of awesome new weapon
systems led to a decreasing need for massive amounts of
military manpower. This, plus the growing dissatisfaction
with the Vietnam War, set the stage for a crucial decision
made in the late sixties and implemented in the early seventies: the decision to end conscription and rely entirely on
volunteers to staff the armed forces.

One of the undesirable side effects of this decision may
have been the exacerbation of two problems: (1) the problem of representativeness, i.e., whether service personnel
reflect a range of demographic characteristics and ideologies nearly as broad as those in the civilian sector; and (2)
the related problem of civilian control of the military, i.e.,
whether military personnel can be counted upon to function in ways that are generally consistent with the ideology
of the civilian population.

The citizen-soldier—the man or woman who enlists
anticipating only a limited period of military service before
returning to civilian life—can be a vital force in dealing
with both of the problems outlined above. Citizen-soldiers
strengthen the linkage between the military sector and the

civilian sector, thus helping to avoid development of a separate military ethos. To the extent that major ideological differences remain between military careerists and the civilian sector, the presence of large numbers of citizen-soldiers within the military may also serve as a valuable corrective—a countervailing influence.

Our review of recent reenlistment data suggests that one-term citizen-soldiers are on the decline, being replaced more and more by those who reenlist and perhaps contemplate military careers. Given our analysis of current trends in civil-military relations, and also given the findings presented in the following chapters, we view this decline of the citizen-soldier with some concern. We do not, however, see it as an inevitable consequence of all-volunteer military staffing. In our final chapter we offer some suggestions for recruiting larger numbers of one-term citizen-soldier volunteers, particularly those whose presence will broaden the range of backgrounds and ideologies within the military and will improve the personnel quality of the armed forces. We consider such an effort to be an important, perhaps essential, step toward ensuring a healthy pattern of civil-military relations during the coming years.

2
A Review of Public Opinion and the Military

As we have already indicated, the public view of the military is a key ingredient in civil-military relations. In this chapter we examine the findings from a number of different surveys that have included questions about various aspects of the military, especially military leadership. Although most of the surveys did not have the military as the primary focus of attention, they provide some very useful perspectives on the ways in which public opinion concerning the military has changed in some respects and has remained surprisingly constant in other respects. In chapter 3 we will continue the examination of civilian views of the military, turning to our own more detailed survey of values and attitudes.

This chapter begins with a look at the crucial factor that influenced recent views concerning the military—the Vietnam War. We will note that there are conflicting views about the military, partly as a consequence of Vietnam; and we will make an effort to sort out and account for some of these conflicts. Then we will look at public views about two aspects of the military which were particularly important during the past decade—the military draft and the defense budget. Finally, we will focus on a review of some data on the ways in which the youth view the military.

Vietnam and the Military

Public attention was focused more and more on the U.S. military during the course of the Vietnam War. Many negative aspects of the military and its personnel were highlighted. These included financial scandals among senior enlisted men, blatant mistreatment of recruits, the specter of widespread drug use, and the nightmare of My Lai-type atrocities of unknown dimensions. These revelations and other factors—the failure to achieve military supremacy despite massive expenditures of resources (both men and material), the increased outrage over the war and the draft, and the growing disaffection with the war as evidenced in the polls—led some scholars to believe that the military had encountered a "problem of legitimacy," and perhaps even a "crisis of legitimacy" (Van Doorn, 1976). In other words, it was felt by some that the disaffection with the war and what it revealed about the military had generalized into disaffection with the military establishment.

It is time to reassess this assumption about what has happened to the public view of the military. Howard Schuman (1972), in his insightful analysis, "Two Sources of Antiwar Sentiment in America," demonstrated empirically that the growing dissent concerning the Vietnam War might be only tangentially related to the sorts of arguments being advanced in the "antiwar movement," especially those expressed on university campuses. He distinguished "moral" opposition to the war from "pragmatic" dissent based on the frustrating expenditure of vast resources coupled with only very meager results of that war. He argued that for most people the growing disaffection with Vietnam did not involve a moral rejection of the war as much as a pragmatic opposition to a costly disappointment. Hence, the generalization of antiwar sentiment to antimilitary sentiment found on campuses might well not be reflected in mass public attitudes toward the military where antiwar sentiment was based primarily on pragmatic considerations rather than moral ones.

In fact, a number of studies at the Institute for Social Research (ISR) at the University of Michigan have found that the mean level of feeling toward the military has been warmer, or more positive, than the mean level toward most other societal groups investigated. A 1973 ISR study had respondents rate a number of institutions on how good a job they were doing for the country as a whole. The U.S. military, along with the nation's colleges and universities, headed the list of fifteen institutions. Sixty percent rated the military as doing a good or very good job, while only 10 percent rated it poor or very poor. In the same study, the people in charge of the military were given one of the highest ratings for being "honest and moral." And when asked whether the military should have more or less influence in society, over one-half of the respondents said it should be "the same as now." The remaining respondents divided almost exactly between those preferring more military influence and those preferring less. No other institution in the study got such evenly balanced ratings of influence (Rodgers and Johnston, 1974).

It has generally been assumed that the public reaction to the Vietnam era affected public views of the military. That has undoubtedly been the case, and our own findings reflect the same. However, it also appears that public feelings over Vietnam have had an impact on the general trust in government. There is considerable evidence to show that the secular trend of trust in government has paralleled that of support for the Vietnam War, i.e., both have decreased remarkably throughout the period from 1964 to the early 1970s (Miller, 1974). This is not to deny that other factors, such as the civil rights movement, urban riots, recessionary periods, inflation, unemployment, and finally Watergate, have been equally or perhaps even more involved in the decline of trust in government. It is to say that pragmatic disaffection with the war might have been directed less toward a military whose hands were dirtied in an *immoral* war and more toward the government which was perceived to have been responsible for an *un-won* war. (See Modigliani, 1972, for a distinction between attitudes about "interventionism" and those dealing with "administration distrust" found among the public during the Korean War.)

Another issue involved in the assumed generalization from revulsion with the horrors of war to antimilitary feelings is the effect of the war on its veterans. The Vietnam Veterans against the War were eloquent spokesmen for the point of view that antiwar sentiment generalized to antimilitary sentiment, but again one must be careful in extrapolating to other Vietnam era veterans. Two separate longitudinal studies which included young veterans, one directed by Jennings and the other directed by Bachman, do not support such an extrapolation (Jennings and Markus, 1974; Bachman and Jennings, 1975). In fact, in the latter study those who went to Vietnam showed an increase in Vietnam dissent but also a moderate increase in support for more money and influence to be given to the military.

This brief discussion of Vietnam and the military indicates that public views about the military and about government in general have been shifting, partly in response to the changing evaluation of U.S. involvement in Vietnam. Next, we will review more than a dozen different surveys carried out in the sixties and seventies, which included data about civilian attitudes toward the military. This review will provide an appropriate temporal context for chapter 3 which presents our own survey of civilian attitudes concerning the military.

Conflicting Views of the Military

There is little consensus among scholars regarding the level of public esteem for the U.S. military. In the summer of 1974, Adam Yarmolinsky (1974) reported the military to be "on the bottom of the scale in national esteem." At the same time, researchers at the University of Michigan were expressing surprise at finding the military to be one of the most trusted public institutions (Rodgers and Johnston, 1974). While we have seen no data that support Yarmolinsky's assertion, two different statistical series show differing trends during the 1964–75 period; high and relatively stable evaluations of the military in one case, and declining public confidence in the other. Analysis of these trends may shed some light on the actual level of public confidence in the military institution.

In the even-numbered years from 1964 to 1974 (with the exception of 1966), the Institute for Social Research asked representative samples of the American population to rate the military and other institutions on a "feeling thermometer" ranging from 0 (very cold or unfavorable) to 100 (very warm or favorable). These data are presented in the first row of table 1. In 1964, the mean rating of the military was 75. The average declined slightly during the following eight years, but had only dropped to 70 in 1972, and was on the increase by 1974. It would appear from these data that the military institution per se was held in high public esteem through the Vietnam War period and in the period thereafter.

Feeling thermometer data were also collected by ISR on evaluations of the Democratic and Republican parties, big business, and labor unions. Row 2 of table 1 presents mean evaluations of these four institutions. Note that these data reveal a modest decline in institutional esteem extending through 1974. Moreover, evaluations of the military were consistently higher than those of each of these comparison institutions taken individually for each year. Indeed, the U.S. findings are not very different from 1974 data from England showing public confidence in the military to be higher than that in most social institutions (*Times*, 1974).

The second statistical series comes from Harris Poll data collected from national samples in 1966 and from 1972 to 1975. Harris asked respondents to indicate their degree of confidence in "the people in charge of" the military and other social institutions. The data on the military are presented in the third row of table 1 and suggest a decrease in confidence during the decade in question. Sixty-two percent

TABLE 1

Trends in Public Attitudes about the Military and Other Institutions

	1964	1965	1966	1967	1968	1969	1970	1971	1972	1973	1974	1975	1976
1. Evaluations of the military (mean ratings)[a]	75				74		73		70		73		
2. Evaluations of four other institutions (mean ratings)[a]	62		62		59				58		56		
3. Confidence in the people in charge of the military (% indicating great confidence)[b]									35	40	33	24	
4. Confidence in the people in charge of four other institutions (% indicating great confidence)[b]			40						22	24	21	15	
5. Support for U.S. involvement in Vietnam (% supporting)[c]		61	51	44	37	32	36						
6. Defense spending (% favoring increased spending)[c]	33					21	8	11					
7. Defense spending (% indicating current level too much)[c]						53		50			44		36

Sources: [a] Institute for Social Research, the University of Michigan
[b] Louis Harris Poll
[c] American Institute of Public Opinion

expressed a great deal of confidence in the people in charge of the military in 1966. This declined markedly to 24 percent in 1975.

Similar data were collected by Harris on confidence in the leaders of major companies and of organized labor, as well as those in the Congress and in the executive branch of the federal government. Mean percentages of people expressing a great deal of confidence in the leaders of these four institutions are presented in row 4 of table 1. The same decline noted for the military is found for these institutions as well. Once again, however, in each year, greater confidence is expressed in the leaders of the military than in the leaders of other institutions. Moreover, this is the case when the military is compared to each of these institutions separately. And while confidence in the leadership of the military has declined by 38 percentage points (as compared to an average decline of 25 percent in the other institutions), the proportional reduction in the two sets of data is equivalent; both showed a drop to roughly three-fifths of the 1966 figures.

Of the two sets of data on the military, one (the ISR "feeling thermometer" ratings) measures affect toward a social institution at a time when confidence in American institutions in general were declining. Interestingly, while part of this general decline has been attributed to the Vietnam War (Miller, 1974), the institution involved in waging the war fared better than did other institutions not involved (compare row 1 with row 2 in table 1). While support for the military institution remained at a high level, public confidence that the United States did the right thing in sending troops to Vietnam declined greatly; the data are presented in row 5 of table 1 (Mueller, 1971). The second set of data on the military measures confidence in the *leaders* of the institution (row 3 in table 1). In this set there seems to be a decline that parallels the decline in support for the Vietnam War. Lipset (1976) has noted the differences in survey responses obtained when respondents are asked to evaluate "the military," the several services, and military leaders.

Who's in Charge?

Part of the apparent contradiction between our two statistical series may be explained by who the leaders of the military are perceived to be. Civil-military relations in the United States are based on an assumption of civilian control (Huntington, 1957). If in fact the public perceives "the people in charge of the military" to be civilians or a combination of military and civilians, then the decline in confidence in these leaders is not inconsistent with the maintenance of high evaluations of the military as an institution.

While we do not have data that explicitly address the question of who is perceived to be in charge of the military, we can approximate such data with responses to a survey conducted in Detroit in 1973 which asked respondents "when a nation gets involved in a war, who is usually most responsible—politicians, the military, or the business community?" Two-thirds of the respondents attributed involvement to politicians. Only 7 percent blamed the military directly, 12 percent blamed the business community, and an equal percentage blamed some combination of these interests. Less than 2 percent of the sample attributed responsibility for war to the three groups combined (Segal, 1976).

Similarly, our own national sample survey conducted in 1973 indicated that Americans perceive civilians to be more influential than military leaders in involving U.S. servicemen in foreign conflicts, as well as in decisions to use nuclear weapons. Military leaders, by contrast, are perceived to be more influential than civilians in matters more internal to the military, i.e., battlefield tactics and the choice of new weapons. In short, decisions affecting the military are perceived to be influenced by both civilian and military leaders. The former, however, are seen to be more responsible for decisions to commit American forces to military engagements, while the latter are more responsible for management decisions made within the context of broader military policy.

Conscription

If the experience of the Vietnam War did not undermine public trust in the military institution, two components of that institution nonetheless did suffer in terms of public opinion—the military draft and the defense budget.

Conscription has been used to raise military manpower in the United States periodically with wide variations in public support, ranging from the New York draft riots during the Civil War to widespread support during World War II. Scholars have noted a long-range secular trend indicating a declining willingness to serve although few quantitative data have been brought to bear on the proposition (Davis, 1974). Analyses over short periods of time suggest increasing support for conscription during World War II, but lower and declining support during 1966 (79 percent) and 1967 (58 percent) (Davis and Dolbeare, 1968).

The continuing decline in support for conscription led us to expect a majority to favor the change to an all-volunteer force. In the 1973 Detroit survey, respondents were asked, "How do you feel about the U.S. replacing the draft with an all-volunteer army?" Seventy-nine percent of our respondents approved or strongly approved of the change—a percentage equal to those who, in a 1966 national sample, favored keeping the draft. Our own 1973 national sample of civilians supported the all-volunteer approach rather than the draft by nearly a two-to-one margin (Bachman, 1973, p. 41).

The Defense Budget

There was a secular decline in public support for defense spending during the Vietnam era (Russett, 1974). Row 6 of table 1 shows the trend for support of more defense spending. The 1973 Detroit sample had been asked, "Out of each federal tax dollar, how many cents would you guess are spent on the military?" Slightly less than 40 cents would have been a good guess. The sample's average guess was slightly less than 30 cents out of each dollar. Our respondents were also asked, "How many cents do you think ought to be spent on the military?" The average response here was still lower, about 16 cents. Slightly less than 60 percent of the respondents felt that less should be spent on the military than they thought was being spent. Eleven percent felt that more should be spent. The remainder felt that the correct amount was being spent. The public's opposition to the magnitude of the defense budget was reflected in other data as well. The respondents had been asked whether they agreed or disagreed with the statement "The people in this country have been asked to make too many sacrifices to support the defense program." Slightly more than 60 percent agreed.

Interestingly, as the Vietnam War became history, and the strength of the U.S. armed forces vis-à-vis those of the Soviet Union became an increasingly salient issue in domestic politics, there was an apparent reversal of the Vietnam era trend. In 1969, 1971, 1974, and 1976, the Gallup Poll asked national samples of Americans, "There is much discussion as to the amount of money the government in Washington should spend for national defense and military purposes. How do you feel about this: do you think we are spending too little, too much, or the right amount?" The percent indicating "too much" decreased at an average rate of 1 to 2 percent a year from 1969 to 1974, and then dropped off markedly, to 36 percent, in spring, 1976 (see row 7, table 1). These percentages are likely to continue to fluctuate in the future due to the influence of the state of the economy, the actual magnitude of the defense budget, the level of international tension, and domestic politics. The recent upswing, at a minimum, supports our contention that the public continues to favor a strong military posture for the United States.

Attitudes of Youth

While a favorable image of the military in the public at large is necessary for the maintenance of the legitimacy of the military institution, the image held by American youth is even more important, for this is the segment of the population that is required, through recruitment, to sustain the institution. One of the impressions left by the Vietnam War was that American youth were opposed to the American military, and indeed, Rodgers and Johnston (1974) do show that respondents aged eighteen to twenty-four rated the military lower than did the rest of the respondents in their national sample. Inglehart (1976), in his 1974 survey data, shows more explicitly increases in positive attitude toward the military with increased age. He found that support of the military on the "feeling thermometer," as well as positive feelings about a son's military service, increased between age eighteen and age sixty-five.

Semiannually between May, 1971, and May, 1974, Gilbert Youth Research, Inc., interviewed representative samples of American male youth aged sixteen to twenty-one on a variety of topics related to the transition to an all-volunteer military force. Included in the questions asked was likelihood of enlisting for active service assuming there was no draft. With the exception of a 3 percent upswing in 1972 (at a time, interestingly enough, when faith in the military institution had declined somewhat in the population at large), the proportion of the age-eligible population likely to enlist was fairly stable at about 12 percent (Goral and Lipowitz, 1975; Goral, 1975).

Additional information concerning youth views of the military is available as a part of a new series of surveys titled "Monitoring the Future: A Continuing Study of the Lifestyles and Values of Youth." The series involves an annual sampling of high school seniors beginning with the class of 1975.[1] In a preliminary analysis of some of the data from the 1975 class, Blair (1977) uncovered several findings which are relevant to our present discussion. One question asked respondents to rate a number of different institu-

---

1. Monitoring the Future is being conducted at the Institute for Social Research under the direction of Lloyd Johnston and Jerald Bachman.

tional settings as possible places to work. The military was given the lowest rating. It was rated as acceptable or desirable by 33 percent of the males and 30 percent of the females. By way of contrast, large corporations and government agencies were both rated as acceptable or desirable by about 60 percent of males and females, and small businesses scored about 75 percent. Blair speculates that most young people see the military as a fine place *for others*—the less fortunate, perhaps. But the perception that the military may be arbitrary and not a good place to get one's ideas heard limits its appeal as a work setting.

Although the military rates lowest among institutional settings as a place to work, the latest Monitoring the Future data (from the class of 1976) show that about 22 percent of the males say they "definitely" or "probably" will serve in the armed forces. The comparable figure for females is a much lower 7 percent. Interestingly enough, when respondents were asked, "Suppose you could do just what you'd like and nothing stood in your way . . . " the proportion of males who checked the military service was 20 percent, but the proportion of females was about 12 percent, much higher than the 7 percent who expected they actually would serve.

The 1976 Monitoring the Future data show a fairly strong association between family socioeconomic level and the likelihood of military service. Among males whose fathers have less than a high school education, about 27 percent expect "probably" or "definitely" to serve, whereas among those males whose fathers completed college, the comparable figure is 17 percent. Among females the overall percentages are lower, of course, but the socioeconomic trend is just as strong. The question asking "Suppose you could do just what you'd like . . . " showed similar socioeconomic trends for both males and females.

The socioeconomic differences in likelihood of military service are substantial, but not nearly so dramatic as the differences by race. Table 2 shows separately responses for white and black males and females. Among males, three times as many blacks as whites say they definitely expect to serve; among females, the disproportion is even greater. The differences for the "Suppose you could do just what you'd like . . . " question are not quite as strong, but they are still very substantial.

Blair's (1977) analysis of Monitoring the Future data for the class of 1975 shows that well over one-half of the males who say they "definitely" will enter the military after high school also expect to be in the service more than a decade later when they are thirty-years old; the comparable figures for females is about one-third. This suggests a rather high proportion of career-oriented individuals among high school seniors planning to join the armed forces.

In sum, these very recent findings from a nationwide survey of high school seniors in 1975 and 1976 show enlistment to be much more likely among blacks and also more likely among people (both black and white) from lower socioeconomic families. In addition, there is a strong indication that a large proportion of new enlistees currently enter the service with military career expectations. Each of these findings is consistent with recent trends in military staffing as noted in the preceding chapter. And, given our view that the all-volunteer force should be demographically representative and should include a substantial proportion of citizen-soldiers, each of these findings gives us some cause for further concern.

Summary and Conclusions

The survey data reviewed in this chapter suggest that there were several dimensions in the public evaluation of the U.S. military establishment during the last decade. As an institution, the military has been highly regarded by the American public, and it retained this regard throughout the Vietnam War period. Confidence in the people *in charge* of the military, by contrast, declined in conjunction with decreased confidence in the leadership of other social institutions, but remained at a high level relative to these other institutions. There are indications that civilian rather than military

TABLE 2

Race and Sex Differences in Perceived Likelihood of Military Service

How likely is it that you will serve in the armed forces after high school?	Males		Females	
	% of White	% of Black	% of White	% of Black
Definitely won't	40	30	75	59
Probably won't	41	27	20	23
Probably will	13	25	4	11
Definitely will	6	18	1	7
Total	100	100	100	100
(Probably + definitely will = total "potential recruits")	19	43	5	18
Suppose you could do just what you'd like and nothing stood in your way. (% marking service in the armed forces as one of the things they would *want* to do.)	19	31	10	21

Source: Monitoring the Future sample of seniors in high school class of 1976 (Institute for Social Research, Johnston and Bachman). N>11,000.

leaders are held responsible for America's involvement in war. Therefore, the decline in confidence in the leaders of the military may, in fact, reflect decreasing faith in the civilians in control, rather than in the military institution.

Concomitant with declining trust in the people in charge of the military, public opinion trends during the late sixties and early seventies reflected the growing opposition to the war in Vietnam, the decrease in support for conscription (which helped bring about the conversion to the all-volunteer force), and the increasing unwillingness during the Vietnam era to support ever-growing defense budgets.

Studies of youth have not indicated a decline in enlistment intentions with the conversion to a volunteer force. However, a very recent survey of high school seniors in 1976 showed disproportionately high enlistment intentions among blacks and among those from lower socioeconomic families. The same study suggested that perhaps as many as one-half or more of those seniors with firm enlistment plans also plan to be in the military at age thirty. Both of these findings have raised concerns about the representativeness of the new all-volunteer force.

Perhaps the most fundamental conclusion to be drawn from the material presented in this chapter is that survey data provide no support for the assertion that the military is or has been at the bottom of the esteem scale relative to other American social institutions. Nor do the data support the view that the esteem of the U.S. military as a whole has declined drastically as a function of the Vietnam experience. On the other hand, concern seems to continue regarding the way policy makers might actually make use of military force.

3

Civilian Views of the Military:
A Closer Look

The previous chapter provided an overview of public views about the military based on a number of different surveys carried out during the period from 1964 through 1976. In this chapter we continue to examine civilian views of the military. However, we take a much more detailed look based upon our nationally representative sample of over 1,800 civilians surveyed in 1973. This study would deserve special attention simply because it covers such a wide range of values, preferences, and perceptions concerning the military. But the primary reason for spotlighting this particular study is that it is one of three surveys, all asking the same questions but to three different groups. Questions that were asked of civilians in early 1973 were also asked of Navy personnel in late 1972 and early 1973, as well as Army personnel in late 1974 and early 1975. In this chapter we . restrict our analysis to the civilian sample; in the next chapter our focus is limited to the military samples; then in chapters 5 and 6 we compare the military and civilian samples, noting both differences and similarities.

This closer look at civilian views of the military addresses a number of questions, including the following:

1. To what extent do attitudes about the military tend to "hang together"? Do people who tend to give the military relatively high marks along one dimension also tend to rate it high in other respects? Is it at all meaningful to think in terms of a single continuum of attitudes about the military ranging from pro-military to antimilitary? For example, would such a continuum be related to attitudes about enlistment?

2. Apart from the question of whether individuals differ in their overall evaluations of the military, are there different aspects of the military that are rated more and less positively? Do some things about the military get high marks from most people while other things about the military get mostly low marks?

3. To what extent do different subgroups within the civilian population hold different views of the military? Do different age groups vary in their evaluations? Are there other differences linked to education? Do veterans, those who have had first-hand experience in the armed forces, differ from non-veterans in their views of the way the military is and the way it ought to be?

The Measures of Values, Preferences, and Perceptions

The survey instrument used for the civilian and military samples consisted of a sixteen-page, self-completed questionnaire. One major segment of the questionnaire dealt exclusively with values, preferences, and perceptions about the U.S. military. The fifty-seven items in this segment were designed to measure a number of different, but interrelated, concepts (the items are reproduced in Appendix E). An important early phase of our analysis involved consolidating these items into a smaller number of variables. This data reduction was intended to serve two purposes. First, it would produce a number of multi-item indexes, which are generally more stable and reliable than single-item measures. Second, it would reduce the complexity of the material to a more manageable level.

Our data reduction efforts included a number of factor analyses which confirmed most of our prior expectations about sets of variables to be combined into indexes, and in a few cases enabled us to isolate items which did not meet our expectations. The analyses were carried out separately for different military and civilian subgroups, and yielded very similar patterns of findings. This indicated that the indexes we developed were applicable across the several groups we studied; moreover, it added to our confidence that the meanings of the questions were basically the same for both civilians and military personnel. The factor analyses are described in greater detail in Appendix B.

The end result of our data reduction is a list of sixteen variables presented in table 3. We attempted to capture the meaning of each variable in a very few words. *In all cases, the variable name corresponds to a high score on the measure.* In the following sections the meanings of the variables in table 3 will become clearer. In addition, Appendix C presents operational definitions of all sixteen variables, including the complete wordings of all questions used.[1]

A General Factor of Military Sentiment

The early explorations of the data indicated that many of our indexes were intercorrelated, thus suggesting a broad continuum or "general factor" of promilitary (or antimilitary) sentiment. In an effort to test that notion, Bachman (1974) performed an additional set of factor analyses based

---

1. The current list of sixteen variables differs slightly from the list of seventeen variables used in a number of our earlier reports (Bachman, 1974; Blair, 1975; Bachman and Blair, 1975; Bachman and Blair, 1976; Blair and Bachman, 1976). One difference is that an index of perceived race and sex discrimination in the military has not been included (for reasons noted later in the text). Additional differences involve the order of the variables and some variable names which have been revised for the sake of clarity. In a few instances the name changes also required that the direction of the scale be reversed.

TABLE 3

Summary of Military Value, Preference, and Perception Measures

	Direction of Loading on General Factor: "Promilitary Sentiment"	Correlation with Views about a Son's Possible Enlistment (N=753 Males)
The Military Organization		
Perceived military job opportunities	+	.29
Perceived fair treatment in services	+	.34
Perceived competence of military leaders	+	.41
Military Obedience		
Servicemen should obey without question	+	.35
Should obey in My Lai-type situation	+	.25
Foreign Policy and Use of Force		
Support for military intervention	+	.20
Preference for U.S. military supremacy	+	.24
Support for U.S. actions in Vietnam	+	.34
Civil-Military Relations		
Role of military seen as positive	+	.34
Preference for higher military spending	+	.34
Perceived military (vs. civilian) influence	−	−.19
Preferred military (vs. civilian) influence	+	.29
Adequacy of military influence (perc.−pref.)	−	−.34
Preference for citizen-soldiers	(−)	−.08
Preferred wide range of views among servicemen	(−)	−.12
Support for amnesty	−	−.34

on the intercorrelations among all of the measures included
in table 3. The analyses were carried out separately for
civilian men, civilian women, and three Navy groups (the
Army data were not yet available when this analysis was
completed). The findings, including the product-moment
correlation matrices, are presented in Bachman's (1974) report. The results of the factor analyses are also detailed in
Appendix B of this volume.

The factor analyses clearly confirmed the view that
there is a substantial general factor of military sentiment
reflected in our data. Table 3 shows the direction of the
loading on this factor for each of our sixteen measures.
(The direction was always the same for all five of the civilian
and military groups analyzed.) Given the data in table 3, let
us consider what it meant (in early 1973) to be at the promilitary end of the continuum. Not surprisingly, those highest in promilitary sentiment gave the military services high
marks for job opportunity and fair treatment, rated military
leaders as quite competent, stated a preference for higher
levels of military spending and influence, and saw the role
of the military in society as predominantly positive. Their
foreign-policy views were rather "hawkish," i.e., they were
relatively supportive of U.S. military intervention in other
countries, they preferred a position of military supremacy
(rather than parity with the USSR), and they were most
likely to support past U.S. involvement in Vietnam. Among
all the dimensions summarized above, the measure of support for U.S. action in Vietnam has a particularly strong
loading on the general factor of military sentiment. Finally,
they placed a high value on obedience to military authority,
that is, they tended to agree that "servicemen should obey
orders without question," and some maintained this position even when faced with a My Lai-type incident.

Two measures which show little association with the
general factor of military sentiment are the dimensions
most closely linked to the debate about the draft versus the
all-volunteer force. These measures are preference for citizen-soldiers (versus "career men") and preference for wide

range of political views among servicemen. Our basic conclusion is that respondents showed little polarization along
these dimensions, possibly indicating that many people had
not given much thought to the issues that these measures
represent.

Views about a Son's Possible Enlistment

One of the most practical reasons for being concerned with
military sentiment among civilians under the new all-volunteer conditions is that the volunteers start out as civilians.
Moreover, they almost always have civilian mothers and
fathers and many civilian friends. These people, sometimes
called significant others, can play a very influential role in
shaping enlistment decisions. With this in mind, we included the following item in the questionnaire, "If you had
a son in his late teens or early twenties who decided to enter
the military service, how would you feel about his decision?"
Response alternatives were "strongly positive, mostly positive, mostly negative, strongly negative." Just over two-
thirds of the civilian respondents faced with this hypotheti-
cal question about a son who had already decided to enter
the service gave a positive answer.

Now the question arises: Do people who hold different
views about the military in general also have different views
about a son's possible enlistment? The findings presented in
the right-hand column of table 3 indicate that they certainly
do. Without exception, every dimension correlates with
feelings about a son's enlistment in the same direction as it
loads on the general factor of military sentiment. (Table 3
shows the findings for civilian males, but the same findings
emerged for five other analysis groups as reported by Bachman, 1974.)

The discussion above has stressed the intercorrelations
among our measures of military views. This pattern has indicated that individuals who were most favorable toward the
military along one dimension tended to be relatively favorable along other dimensions. But this does not mean that for

a typical individual, or for the public in general, views about the military were consistently positive or consistently negative. On the contrary, there were substantial differences in overall ratings of the several aspects of the military that we explored. Along some dimensions the dominant public view was quite favorable, while along others it was not. We now turn our attention to some of the differences.

Rating Different Aspects of the Military

Figure 1 presents a profile summary of the ratings that the civilian sample supplied for each of the sixteen measures of military views. In this figure, and several others to follow, we have found it useful to represent all sixteen measures along a single scale of military sentiment. Let us describe briefly the procedure we selected. Given sixteen measures based on different numbers of items, that is, items with several different response scales, midpoints, and ranges, the use of a single overall scale of military sentiment requires that we make some arbitrary decisions. For each measure, we treat the midpoint of the range of possible scores as representing a "neutral point," a position which does not seem especially favorable or unfavorable toward the military. Using this method, we can examine the mean score for an analysis group and see whether it is to the promilitary side of the neutral point (shown on the right) or the antimilitary side (shown on the left). In order to scale the distances away from the neutral point in a way that provides some comparability across the sixteen measures, we express each departure from the midpoint as a fraction of the standard deviation (SD) for the measure in question. Thus, for example, the mean score for civilians on the measure of perceived military job opportunities was (in 1973) 3.40, or .40 above the neutral point of 3.00 for that measure. The standard deviation for that measure is .89, so .40 represents 44 percent of a standard deviation. Accordingly, we express the mean score for all civilians as .44 scale units toward the promilitary end of the continuum. (In order to facilitate comparisons among groups, all other figures of this type use the standard deviation for the total civilian sample as the basis for computing departures from the neutral point.)[2]

The findings reported in figure 1 provide a somewhat different perspective on civilian images of the military. We reported above that the sixteen dimensions of military views are highly interrelated and display a common underlying factor. But now when we look at mean scores rather than correlations, we can also see that in early 1973 the public was neither predominantly promilitary nor primarily anti-military. The public *as a whole* evaluated different aspects of the military quite differently, even though each measure may order *individuals* similarly.

As the four headings in figure 1 suggest, we have found it useful to distinguish several fundamentally different aspects of the military that were evaluated by the public

---

2. One can, of course, quarrel with this approach of converting mean scores for all sixteen dimensions into promilitary deviation scores. Some of the dimensions correlate more strongly with the general factor of military sentiment than do others, yet we have not taken this into account in our scaling procedures. Further, the selection of the midpoint of each scale as the point we interpret as substantively neutral is subject to argument in at least some cases. Finally, it is not at all clear that the standard deviation for the total civilian sample should be used to scale scores of particular civilian subgroups, much less military groups. (In fact, some of our earlier work followed the more complex approach of using the standard deviation of the particular group under analysis as the basis for scaling. Fortunately, the conclusions are essentially the same whether we use the complex or the more simple approach!)

Our defense in each case is that the procedure we have followed is the least complicated one we could devise and still accomplish our purposes. Moreover, although our relatively simple rules for scaling may miss some subtleties, they are at least applied evenhandedly to all scales. (Had we tried to introduce our subjective judgments to develop a more "ideal" scaling procedure, it would have been hard to know where to stop, and harder still to justify to someone else with different subjective judgments.) Our decision to use the civilian standard deviations as the basis for scaling all of the deviation scores reflects our treatment of civilian values and attitudes as the starting point for this investigation, that is, whether the views of military personnel show significant departures from civilian views.

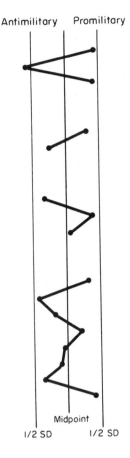

Antimilitary   Promilitary

The Military Organization
   Perceived military job opportunities
   Perceived fair treatment in services
   Perceived competence of military leaders

Military Obedience
   Servicemen should obey without question
   Should obey in My Lai-type situation

Foreign Policy and Use of Force
   Support for military intervention
   Preference for U.S. military supremacy
   Support for U.S. actions in Vietnam

Civil-Military Relations
   Role of military seen as positive
   Preference for higher military spending
   Perceived military (vs. civilian) influence
   Preferred military (vs. civilian) influence
   Adequacy of military influence (perc.—pref.)
   Preference for citizen-soldiers
   Preferred wide range of views among servicemen
   Support for amnesty

Midpoint

1/2 SD   1/2 SD

Fig. 1. Profile of civilian views about the military. The data used to construct this figure are presented in table 16 in Appendix D.

and reflected by these findings. These aspects include the military organization, military obedience, foreign policy and the use of force, and a collection of other measures that have to do with civil-military relations. We do not present these four categories as any sort of formal theoretical framework. Our purpose is simply to organize our findings in a meaningful way (and, hopefully, one that is consistent with some of the literature and issues discussed earlier).

The Military Organization

The first three measures listed in figure 1 deal with aspects of the military as an organization: the job opportunities it provides; the extent to which it provides fair treatment; and, perhaps most importantly, the competence of its leadership. Along two of these dimensions the public view of the military was mostly positive, but perceptions about fair treatment in the service were less favorable. Let us look at each of these measures in more detail.

The measure of perceived job opportunities is an index based on five questions, each of which asked respondents to rate the extent to which certain opportunities are available to people who work in the military services. The lowest ratings were given to the item "A chance to get their ideas heard." The mean rating for this item was 2.75 (on a scale where 2 means "to a little extent," 3 means "to some extent," and 4 means "to a great extent"). Higher ratings were given to "A chance to have a personally more fulfilling job" (3.34), "A chance to advance to a more responsible position" (3.64), and "A chance to get more education" (3.85).

In sum, most civilians in 1973 perceived the military as providing quite good educational opportunities and fairly good chances to take on responsibilities, get ahead, and have a personally fulfilling job. However, the military was not seen as a very good place to get one's own ideas heard. It is worth mentioning that earlier analyses of these data (Bachman, 1973) found the same ranking of these five dimensions among Navy officers and also enlisted men. The similarities among rankings suggest that there is an underlying reality which is being perceived accurately. If not, then there is at least a stereotype of military job opportunities that is pervasive enough to be held not only by civilians, but also by enlisted men and officers.

The second measure shown in figure 1 deals with fair treatment in the military and is based on two items. The first asked, "To what extent is it likely that a person in the military can get things changed and set right if he is being unjustly treated by a superior?" The mean response for civilians was 2.46, midway between "a little extent" and "some extent." The second item asked, "Do you personally feel that *you* would receive more just and fair treatment as a civilian or as a member of the military service?" The mean rating by all civilians fell almost exactly midway between "about the same" and "more fair as a civilian." Only 10 percent of the respondents thought treatment would be *more* fair in the military than as a civilian, while 44 percent thought treatment would be less fair in the military. The two items thus yield the same basic conclusion: the military does not receive high ratings as a place for fair treatment. Note that this fits quite well with the perception that the military is not a very good place for getting one's ideas heard.

Two other measures dealing with fair treatment in the military have not been included in figure 1 or in our list of sixteen dimensions because we could not decide on an appropriate neutral point (and we were not at all comfortable with using the midpoint of the scale as a neutral point for these items). One question asked, "To what extent do you think there is any discrimination against women who are in the armed services?" The mean response fell midway between "a little extent" and "some extent" for both civilian men (2.52) and civilian women (2.61). The other question was couched in similar terms, "To what extent do you think there is any discrimination against black people who are in the armed services?" Here again the responses fell midway between "a little extent" and "some extent" and were virtually identical for civilian men (2.46) and civilian women (2.45). A further analysis of this item is worth quoting:

> Looking separately at white and black Navy respondents, we find the median rating by whites is that discrimination against blacks exists in the services "to a little extent," while the median rating by blacks is that anti-black discrimination exists "to a great extent." At first blush, this might suggest that black Navy men find the military services unattractive. But when we compare black and white Navy enlisted men's ratings of just and fair treatment in military service versus civilian life, we find that blacks are more favorable toward military service than are whites. The black enlisted men, on the average, rate chances for fair treatment in the military service as being "about the same" as those in civilian life. In other words, while blacks in the Navy perceive a considerable amount of racial discrimination in the military services, they apparently see it as no worse than the level of discrimination they would be exposed to as civilians. (Bachman, 1973, p. 12)

It appears, in retrospect, that we should have included an item for all respondents asking whether blacks (and perhaps also women) are likely to receive fairer treatment (or less discrimination) in the military or in civilian life. The absence of this form of question plus the complexities of interpretation illustrated above led us to the conclusion that we did not have an adquate measure of discrimination to be included in our list of views about the military. Nevertheless, the findings noted above do enrich our understanding of civilian perceptions about fair treatment in the military.

The third measure dealing with the military organization, as shown in figure 1, involves perceptions about the competence of military leaders. Two items were selected to form this index. The first asked, "To what extent do you think our military leaders are smart people who know what they are doing?" The mean response was 3.33, between "some extent" (scored 3) and "a great extent" (scored 4). The second question asked, "To what extent do you think you can trust our military leadership to do what is right?" The mean response was slightly higher at 3.46. The responses to these two items suggest that civilian confidence in military leadership was at a *moderately* positive level in 1973.

Military Obedience

One of the fundamental distinctions between military and civilian life is that a high degree of obedience can be demanded from military personnel. The My Lai massacre brought this issue into sharp focus and raised the question of when servicemen should properly refuse to obey an order. Several of our questionnaire items, adapted from the work of Kelman and Lawrence (1972), were based explicitly upon the My Lai events.

First, let us consider a more general item which states the matter of obedience in abstract but extremely simple terms: "Servicemen should obey orders without question." The majority of civilians in 1973, about 70 percent, said they agree or "agree mostly" with this statement.

The next question in the sequence presented a specific instance patterned after the My Lai events: "Suppose a group of soldiers in Vietnam had been ordered by their superior officers to shoot all inhabitants of a village suspected of aiding the enemy, including old men, women, and children? In your opinion, what should soldiers do in such a situation?" The question provided three response possibilities: "Follow orders and shoot; refuse to shoot them; don't know." Among civilian men, 28 percent indicated that the soldiers should follow orders and shoot, 39 percent said they should refuse, and the rest didn't know. Among women, only 15 percent thought they should shoot, 36 percent thought they should refuse, and fully 49 percent said they didn't know what the soldiers should do in such a situation.

Both of the obedience items described above are included in our list of sixteen measures, and in each case a high score on the measure indicates high support for obedience. As table 3 indicates, both obedience items are positively related to the general factor of military sentiment (and, as the data in Appendix B show, the factor loadings are quite strong). This means that those who are generally most favorable toward the military are also most likely to say that soldiers should obey orders.

Before moving on to our next topic area, it may be useful to mention the other items dealing with obedience in a My Lai-type situation, although these items are not included among our sixteen measures of attitudes about the military. The work of Kelman and Lawrence (1972), which served as a stimulus and model for our own questions about obedience, involved a national sample of nearly a thousand people interviewed in late May and early June of 1971, about two months after the conviction of Lieutenant William Calley for his actions in the My Lai massacre. The two questions from the 1971 study which are of particular interest to us were worded, "What would most people do if ordered to shoot all inhabitants of a Vietnamese village suspected of aiding the enemy, including old men, women, and children?" and "What would you do in this situation?" In answer to the first question, fully 67 percent of the Kelman and Lawrence sample thought that most people would follow orders and shoot; 19 percent thought most people would refuse, and an additional 14 percent gave other answers or no opinion. Perhaps more shocking are the answers to the second question: 51 percent thought they themselves would follow orders and shoot, 33 percent thought they would refuse, and 16 percent gave other responses. Kelman and Lawrence caution against the assumption that "refuse to shoot" was clearly the socially desirable response in their interview situation. They suggest that many of the 51 percent who said they would follow orders and shoot may have considered it their moral obligation to do so.

The Kelman and Lawrence survey did not include a question about what *should* be done in a My Lai-type situation, but our adaptation of the question sequence did. As we noted above, 28 percent of the men and 15 percent of the women thought the soldiers should follow orders and shoot, while 39 percent of the men and 36 percent of the women said the soldiers should refuse to shoot. We then asked our respondents two more questions which very closely paralleled the Kelman and Lawrence ones, "What do you think most people would actually do if they were in this situation?" and "What do you think you would do in this situation?" Compared to the 1971 sample used by Kelman and Lawrence, our own sample of civilians showed smaller, but still quite substantial, proportions selecting the "follow orders and shoot" response to both questions.

In response to the question about what they themselves would do in such a situation, 39 percent of the men and 44 percent of the women in our sample said they would refuse to shoot, figures that are slightly higher than the 33 percent Kelman and Lawrence found for their total sample. Much more important are the differences in those who said they would follow orders and shoot. While the earlier study based on the 1971 sample found 51 percent in this category, our own 1973 sample had 29 percent of the civilian men in this category and a very low 13 percent of the women.

Do these differences between our findings and those of Kelman and Lawrence reflect differences in methodology (most of which were unavoidable)? Or does it show a shift in national opinion over the two-year period from 1971 to 1973? Given the direction of the change, it is tempting to attribute it entirely to a shift in national views about proper military conduct. However, there is some likelihood that the question format, including the oft chosen "don't know" category, played some role in the shift. Nonetheless, we think that the format is a reasonable one, and we suspect that at least some of the difference between the 1971 and 1973 samples reflects a real shift in attitudes away from what might have been partly a "sympathy vote" for Lieutenant Calley. (A comparison of the 1972–73 Navy data with the 1974–75 Army data suggests that attitudes may have continued to change, as we shall note in later chapters.)

Foreign Policy and the Use of Force

When is war justified? Most people would agree that the most fundamental reason for going to war would be to defend against an attack upon one's own country, and many would add that a strong military force is necessary as a deterrent against such an attack. Our survey included a number of items dealing with these issues. Three indexes based on these items have been included in figure 1.

The first index is based on two items using an agree-disagree response format. Nearly equal proportions of the civilian population agreed and disagreed with the statement in the first of these questions, "There may be times when the U.S. should go to war to protect the rights of other countries." But fully three-fourths agreed with the second question, which stated the issue in the opposite direction, "The only good reasons for the U.S. to go to war is to defend against an attack on our own country." When we combined these two items into an index, we found that the civilian population as a whole could be characterized as not very favorable toward military intervention on behalf of other countries. Seventy percent, however, agreed with another item, "The U.S. should be willing to go to war to protect its own economic interests."

The second index, which deals with views about the need for U.S. military supremacy, is also based on two agree-disagree items. Two-thirds disagreed with the statement, "The U.S. does not need to have greater military power than the Soviet Union." Consistently enough, the majority agreed with the statement in the next question, "The U.S. ought to have much more military power than any other nation in the world." In short, the more dominant preference among civilians was for some degree of military supremacy.

We discussed earlier the fact that our decade of involvement in Southeast Asia has been an important, perhaps the dominant, factor shaping recent attitudes toward the military, especially views about the use of military force to deal with the problems of other countries. Our measure of support for U.S. action in Vietnam did not, in early 1973, show the overwhelming rejection of the Vietnam War generally reported in poll findings. We suspect this was the case because we did not simply ask respondents whether the war was a mistake, but instead asked a series of questions that contained both "moral" and "pragmatic" considerations. Unfortunately, these measures had been developed long before Schuman's (1972) seminal work appeared, and the moral and pragmatic aspects of sentiment toward the war were not clearly delineated in our questions.

A detailed analysis of the findings for the Vietnam items is presented in an earlier work (Bachman, 1973). A brief summary will be sufficient for our present purposes. There was somewhat more agreement than disagreement with statements that the war had been damaging to our national honor or pride, and that it had not really been in the national interest. But there was also somewhat more agreement than disagreement that our fighting in Vietnam had been important (*a*) to fight the spread of Communism, (*b*) to protect friendly countries, and (*c*) to show other nations that we keep our promises. In short, civilian appraisals of U.S. action in Vietnam were mixed.

Civil-Military Relations

The remaining eight of our sixteen measures are grouped loosely under the general rubric of civil-military relations. All of them have to do in one way or another with the relationship between the military institution and the larger civilian society. The first of these measures is a single global issue evaluating the role of the military as positive or negative, "Overall, how do you feel about the role of the military services in our society during the time since World War II—

has it been mostly positive or mostly negative?" Two-thirds rated the contribution as positive. More specifically, 8 percent checked "strongly positive," 61 percent "mostly positive," 26 percent "mostly negative," and 5 percent "strongly negative."

Another more specific aspect of civil-military relations has to do with the willingness to spend money on the military. Our measure of preference for higher military spending consisted of the question, "Do you think the U.S. spends too much or too little on the armed services?" The following response alternatives were provided: "Far too much" (scored 1), "too much" (2), "about right" (3), "too little" (4), "far too little" (5). Only 13 percent of the respondents felt that too little was being spent on the military, 45 percent considered the amount about right, and a substantial 42 percent thought that too much was being spent. The mean score for all civilians in 1973 was 2.59, roughly midway on the scale between "about right" and "too much."

Another aspect of civil-military relations involves influence over various decisions affecting national security. These decisions range from battlefield tactics to the use of nuclear weapons. In chapter 6 we will treat this topic at length; for the present we will only introduce three indexes that deal with military versus civilian influence. Five pairs of questions asked respondents to rate military and civilian influence in different areas. Each pair of questions asked the respondent first to mark "This is how I think it is now," and then to mark "This is how I'd like it to be." Response categories range from "civilian leaders much more influence" (scored 1) through "about equal influence" (3) to "military leaders much more influence" (5). The index of perceived military (versus civilian) influence is based on the five ratings of " . . . how I think it is now." The index of preferred military (versus civilian) influence is based on the five ratings of " . . . how I'd like it to be." One other index, called adequacy of military influence (perceived minus preferred), is based on the discrepancy between perceived and preferred influence. If the perceived level of influence is equal to what is preferred, then military influence would be adequate. If perception is greater than preference, then military influence is considered to be excessive. If a respondent, however, prefers more military influence than he perceives actually exists, then his adequacy score is low.

It is evident in table 3 that these three indexes are related in different ways to the general factor of military sentiment. Those who were generally most favorable toward the military were also most likely to prefer relatively high levels of military influence. We would naturally expect this kind of relationship with preferences. But what is interesting is that the perceptions of actual military versus civilian influence are also related to general military attitudes, but in the opposite direction. The more favorable someone felt toward the military in general, the more likely he was to rate the actual amounts of influence by military (versus civilian) leaders as rather low. It follows, then, that those most favorable toward the military tended to see the current levels of military influence as inadequate, i.e., the levels they perceived were lower than the levels they preferred.

For civilians as a whole, mean preferences for military versus civilian influence were just about identical to mean perceptions of actual influence levels, suggesting that in 1973 there was a good deal of satisfaction with the status quo. Such average data may be a bit misleading since at the individual level there was a good deal of variability in views about the adequacy of military influence. Some perceived actual levels of military influence to be much higher than they preferred, while others took just the opposite view. As we shall soon see, some of these differences are related to age, education, and prior military experience.

The remaining three measures that we have classified under the heading of civil-military relations have to do with those who serve in the armed forces and what happens to those who refuse to serve. The index of preference for citizen-soldiers was based on two questions using the agree-disagree format. The first item was worded as follows,

"Most of our servicemen should be 'citizen-soldiers'—men who spend just three or four years in the service." Sixty-two percent of the respondents agreed or "agreed mostly" with this item. The next item presented the other side of the issue, "Our military service should be staffed mostly with 'career men' who spend twenty or more years in the service." Nevertheless, there was only very limited consistency in responses to the two items (the product-moment correlation for civilians is −.22). Responses to the second item were divided almost equally between those who agreed and those who disagreed. This index showed a slight negative association with overall military sentiment. Those most favorable toward the military in general were a bit less likely than average to favor citizen-soldiers.

Another index based on two agree-disagree items dealt with the matter of a "separate military ethos" or the notion that military men might tend toward some common political point of view. One item stated the case for having a variety of political viewpoints, "There ought to be a wide range of different political viewpoints among those in the military service." This statement was endorsed by over two-thirds of the civilian respondents. The other item in the index stated a different (if not opposite) view, "Only those who agree with our military policy should be allowed to serve in the armed forces." Just over one-half (53 percent) disagreed with this statement; but opinions were more mixed than might have been expected given the responses to the other item in the index. Perhaps some respondents felt that military men could agree with military policy and still show a wide range of different political viewpoints. (The responses to the two items correlate only -.07.) This index, like the previous one, showed a slight negative relationship with overall military sentiment; those most promilitary were a bit less eager to see a wide range of political viewpoints among service personnel.

The last measure was an index of support for amnesty. Views about amnesty comprised an important part of the climate of opinion about the military in 1973. In addition, amnesty was an issue in the 1976 presidential campaign. Amnesty was strongly (and negatively) linked to overall feelings about the military and it showed one of the sharpest age polarizations to appear in these data.

Once again the index consisted of two agree-disagree items, one stated in positive terms and the other in negative terms. The negative-termed item was presented first, "Going to Canada to avoid fighting in Vietnam was wrong, and those who did so should be punished." Two-thirds of the civilians agreed or "agreed mostly" with this statement. The next item presented the case positively, "The men who went to Canada rather than fight in Vietnam were doing what they felt was right. They should be allowed to return to the U.S. without being punished." Two-thirds disagreed with this item. Responses to these two items showed a very high level of consistency; the product-moment correlation was −.75 for the civilian sample. It appears that for this dimension, unlike the ones dealing with citizen-soldiers and different political views, the respondents knew where they stood on the issue and their stand was highly consistent. As we noted above, this index was also strongly linked to overall views about the military; those most promilitary were least supportive of amnesty.

We have come to the end of our overview of the measures displayed in figure 1. We have dwelt on them at length partly because we wanted to capture in some detail the range of civilian views about the military in 1973, and partly because we will be using them a good deal more in this chapter and in chapters 4 and 5.

We have examined four broad categories of views about the military: the military organization, military obedience, foreign policy and the use of force, and civil-military relations. In each of these areas we have found that civilians in 1973 were in some respects predominantly positive and in other respects more negative. Now we turn to some subgroups of civilians where the viewpoints lie more consistently to one side or the other of the neutral point.

Differences among Subgroups

Thus far we have looked at the distribution of respondents' values, perceptions, and preferences only at the aggregate level. During the Vietnam War, Americans became sensitized to the counterculture expressed among youth, and to the quite different attitudes displayed by "hard hats." These reactions to the Vietnam War and to "the military" suggest that if we look only at the average civilian's view, we will miss some very important differences in perspectives on the military. There are several possible bases of cleavage within the civilian population that may be important in examining these issues.

In earlier analyses we examined age, education, sex, race, region of the country, and size of community as factors which might be related to military views. Age and education are linked to some substantial differences, as we shall see. But the other dimensions yielded relatively few differences (Blair, 1975; Bachman and Blair, 1975). In particular, it is worth noting that the responses of males and females in the civilian sample were found to be similar in nearly all respects (see Bachman, 1973 and 1974 for further details). This is important because our analyses of Navy and Army samples are limited to males. The absence of any substantial sex differences in the civilian sample means that it makes virtually no difference whether the military samples are compared with all civilians or with civilian males only.

Variation by Age and Education

Given that the other demographic variables we explored were found to be of lesser importance, we can now concentrate our attention on the dimensions of age and education. Table 4 presents mean scores for six age groups. As the data in the table indicate, the relationship of age to the measures under consideration is not neatly linear. Youth aged sixteen to eighteen generally presented a more positive view of the military than did those aged nineteen to twenty-four. The latter group was the most negative age range of all. The same negative pattern appeared, but to a lesser extent, among those aged twenty-five to thirty-four. The group of adults most positive toward various aspects of the military were those aged thirty-five to forty-four. This group had the largest proportion of views reminiscent of the cold war, i.e., the greatest support for military intervention, in contrast to the more isolationist views of those both younger and older.

It is of interest to examine a few other specific dimensions of military views, particularly to note those which are strongly related to age. The right-hand column in table 4 presents the correlation ratio, eta (adjusted for degrees of freedom), which shows both linear and nonlinear association between age and each of our sixteen measures. The two strongest relationships involve views concerning servicemen obeying orders without question, and views concerning amnesty for those who refused to fight in Vietnam. In the case of amnesty, the relationship is almost perfectly linear: the older the respondent, the less support there was for amnesty (and the stronger the feeling that those who avoided fighting in Vietnam should be punished). The views about obedience also showed a linear relationship with age with the one exception noted earlier. Beginning with age nineteen, the older the respondent, the more likely he was to agree that servicemen should obey orders without question. However, the youngest respondents (age sixteen to eighteen) were at an intermediate point in their support for obedience.

In sum, age is an important source of variation for a number of the views we are examining. The fact that most of the relationships are not simply straight lines suggests that the military attitudes of different age cohorts have been shaped somewhat permanently by the various major events through which they have lived.

The relationships with education, as shown in table 5, are much more straightforward: the higher the level of education, the less favorable the attitudes toward the mili-

TABLE 4

Mean Scores for Civilian Age Groups

	Age						Correlation Ratio, Eta (adj)
	16-18 (N=109)	19-24 (N=249)	25-34 (N=403)	35-44 (N=272)	45-60 (N=425)	≥61 (N=301)	
The Military Organization							
Perceived military job opportunities	3.54	3.38	3.27	3.36	3.46	3.48	.086
Perceived fair treatment in services	2.62	2.38	2.37	2.52	2.49	2.61	.088
Perceived competence of military leaders	3.36	3.07	3.28	3.51	3.53	3.55	.178
Military Obedience							
Servicemen should obey without question	2.71	2.34	2.58	2.91	3.01	3.23	.297
Should obey in My Lai-type situation	1.73	1.68	1.79	1.91	1.87	1.91	.095
Foreign Policy and Use of Force							
Support for military intervention	2.33	2.20	2.31	2.49	2.15	2.07	.162
Preference for U.S. military supremacy	2.69	2.57	2.76	2.96	3.02	2.95	.172
Support for U.S. actions in Vietnam	2.57	2.36	2.48	2.65	2.59	2.62	.119
Civil-Military Relations							
Role of military seen as positive	2.70	2.47	2.75	2.83	2.74	2.78	.150
Preference for higher military spending	2.69	2.48	2.48	2.65	2.68	2.65	.081
Perceived military (vs. civilian) influence	3.51	3.52	3.23	2.98	3.10	3.11	.160
Preferred military (vs. civilian) influence	3.15	3.06	3.08	3.26	3.27	3.25	.093
Adequacy of military influence (perc.−pref.)	4.37	4.46	4.15	3.72	3.82	3.87	.191
Preference for citizen-soldiers	2.79	2.72	2.64	2.49	2.55	2.48	.107
Preferred wide range of views among servicemen	2.75	2.89	2.86	2.78	2.75	2.61	.098
Support for amnesty	2.63	2.61	2.08	1.79	1.81	1.86	.283

tary. There is also a somewhat greater consistency across measures in the case of education than was true for age. Each of the measures dealing with the military organization shows the relationship with education, and so do both measures dealing with military obedience. In the area of foreign policy and the use of force, there is no relationship between education and support for military intervention to protect other countries. We do find, however, that those with greater amounts of education were less supportive of U.S. military supremacy and of U.S. actions in Vietnam.

In the area of civil-military relations the linkages with education vary in strength, although the pattern is consistent in showing college graduates as least promilitary. The dimensions which show the effect most strongly are support for military spending and preference for higher levels of military influence; in both cases the college graduates tended to prefer less.

One of the reasons for our interest in age and education as factors linked to military attitudes within the civilian population is the fact that both of these dimensions vary among the military subgroups we will be examining in the next chapter. Officers are better educated than enlisted men, on the average. Career military men tend to be older (or cover a wider age range) than noncareer servicemen. Thus, in chapter 5 when we compare various categories of military men and their civilian counterparts, we will define those counterparts in terms of age and education.

Before leaving this comparison of age and education groups in the civilian population, it will be useful to present a graphic summary of the differences in military viewpoints as they were evidenced in our 1973 sample. In an earlier report we dichotomized our sample into "younger" (age 34 and below) and "older" (age 35 and above) categories, and we also separated the sample into college graduates and those with less than a college degree. These two dichotomies taken together gave us four analysis groups. We found that the younger college graduates were consistently the least supportive of the military, while the older nongradu-

TABLE 5

Mean Scores for Civilian Educational Groups

	Education				Correlation Ratio, Eta (adj)
	Less Than 12 Years (N=574)	12 Years (N=580)	Some College (N=316)	College Graduate (N=243)	
The Military Organization					
Perceived military job opportunities	3.59	3.40	3.22	3.12	.188
Perceived fair treatment in services	2.69	2.52	2.30	2.13	.225
Perceived competence of military leaders	3.57	3.43	3.20	3.16	.166
Military Obedience					
Servicemen should obey without question	3.03	2.83	2.62	2.50	.186
Should obey in My Lai-type situation	1.94	1.87	1.73	1.62	.147
Foreign Policy and Use of Force					
Support for military intervention	2.20	2.23	2.32	2.27	.032
Preference for U.S. military supremacy	3.02	2.91	2.75	2.44	.210
Support for U.S. actions in Vietnam	2.65	2.58	2.45	2.30	.158
Civil-Military Relations					
Role of military seen as positive	2.77	2.78	2.64	2.56	.115
Preference for higher military spending	2.79	2.63	2.48	2.22	.204
Perceived military (vs. civilian) influence	3.24	3.17	3.22	3.13	*
Preferred military (vs. civilian) influence	3.32	3.25	3.08	2.83	.194
Adequacy of military influence (perc.−pref.)	3.92	3.93	4.15	4.30	.100
Preference for citizen-soldiers	2.66	2.56	2.58	2.46	.077
Preferred wide range of views among servicemen	2.66	2.78	2.89	3.00	.155
Support for amnesty	2.03	1.89	2.18	2.30	.124

*Adjusted value is less than zero.

ates were most promilitary. Our earlier report (Blair and
Bachman, 1976) presented all four of the age/education
groups, and we have included data for all four groups in
the appendix of this volume (table 17). However, for purposes of clarity, the display in figure 2 shows only the two
extreme groups, the younger college graduates and the
older nongraduates.

The figure shows quite clearly that the differences between the two groups appear along every dimension except
the one having to do with military intervention to protect
other countries. On the other two measures dealing with
foreign policy and the use of force, the differences are particularly large. With only a few exceptions, the younger college graduates showed a majority on the negative side of
the neutral point of each scale. They were particularly critical of fair treatment in the services, and they were also
likely to see military spending as too high. The majority of
the older nongraduates were to the positive side of most
scales, but on a number of dimensions (including those just
mentioned) the majority were on the negative side. It is
especially noteworthy that this subgroup of civilians who
were positive toward the military in many respects were,
nevertheless, doubtful about the extent to which those in
the military are likely to get treated as fairly as civilians are.

Veterans' Views of the Military

There are a number of ways by which people form attitudes
about the military. But firsthand personal contacts may
have a much greater impact and credibility. Thus it seemed
useful to explore the degree to which the various perceptions and attitudes about the military and its mission were
linked to such personal contacts.

In this section we will explore firsthand military contacts among the civilian men in our sample. First, we will see
to what extent civilian men who had served in the armed
forces differed from those who had not. Second, we will
explore the extent to which positive or negative feelings

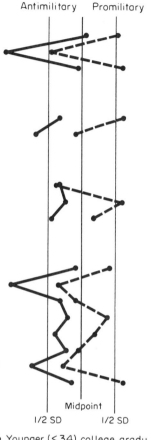

The Military Organization
    Perceived military job opportunities
    Perceived fair treatment in services
    Perceived competence of military leaders

Military Obedience
    Servicemen should obey without question
    Should obey in My Lai-type situation

Foreign Policy and Use of Force
    Support for military intervention
    Preference for U.S. military supremacy
    Support for U.S. actions in Vietnam

Civil-Military Relations
    Role of military seen as positive
    Preference for higher military spending
    Perceived military (vs. civilian) influence
    Preferred military (vs. civilian) influence
    Adequacy of military influence (perc.—pref.)
    Preference for citizen-soldiers
    Preferred wide range of views among servicemen
    Support for amnesty

Antimilitary   Promilitary

Midpoint
1/2 SD   1/2 SD

●——● Younger (≤ 34) college graduates
●– –● Older (≥ 35) nongraduates

Fig. 2. Comparison of civilian age and education groups. The data used to construct this figure are presented in tables 16 and 17 in Appendix D.

about past military service were related to military attitudes and perceptions.

Is the average veteran more supportive of the military than the average nonveteran? Our data, summarized in column *A* of table 6, indicate few differences between the average veteran and nonveteran along our dimensions, and those differences which do appear are not very large. When asked how they would feel about a son's enlistment, 29 percent of the veterans answered "strongly positive," compared to 23 percent of the nonveterans; those responding "mostly positive" were 45 percent and 46 percent, respectively. Differences this small are neither statistically trustworthy nor substantively important (they correspond to a point-biserial correlation of .08).

Reviewing the figures in column *A* of table 6, we find no average differences between veterans and nonveterans in their perceptions of the military work role or the competence of military leaders, and no substantial differences in their views about foreign policy and military power. In ratings of ideal levels of military versus civilian influence, there was little difference between the two groups; both veterans and nonveterans preferred a roughly equal sharing of influence by military and civilian leaders. However, there was a difference in perceptions of actual levels of military influence. Veterans perceived the military as somewhat less influential than the nonveterans. As a result, the two groups differed along our dimension of adequacy of military influence. Veterans preferred more military influence than they felt was actually the case, whereas nonveterans preferred slightly less.

It is interesting to note that the veterans' scores along the military versus civilian influence dimensions were quite similar to those of first-term enlisted men, as we shall see in the next chapter. It may be that one of the most consistent results of past or present experience in military service is a lowered assessment of the amount of influence that military leaders actually have over a range of decisions affecting national security.

TABLE 6
Impact of Past Military Service on Attitudes of Civilian Men

	Correlations with	*A. Past Military Service* (All Civilian Men, N=719)	*B. Positive Feelings about Having Served* (Veterans Only, N=349)
The Military Organization			
Perceived military job opportunities		.00	.18
Perceived fair treatment in services		.02	.33
Perceived competence of military leaders		.02	.31
Military Obedience			
Servicemen should obey without question		.04	.35
Should obey in My Lai-type situation		.09	.29
Foreign Policy and Use of Force			
Support for military intervention		.10	.18
Preference for U.S. military supremacy		.07	.18
Support for U.S. actions in Vietnam		.07	.32
Civil-Military Relations			
Role of military seen as positive		.05	.34
Preference for higher military spending		.07	.33
Perceived military (vs. civilian) influence		−.23	−.17
Preferred military (vs. civilian) influence		.07	.25
Adequacy of military influence (perc.−pref.)		−.23	−.30
Preference for citizen-soldiers		−.18	−.08
Preferred wide range of views among servicemen		.06	−.10
Support for amnesty		−.19	−.36

Note: The correlations are product-moment. However, the "past military service" variable is a dichotomy, and thus the correlations in column *A* are also termed point-biserial. (The point-biserial is a special case of the product-moment correlation. In the present instance it can be interpreted in essentially the same way as the more typical product-moment correlation involving continuous distributions along both dimensions.) Correlations in column *A* may be considered statistically significant if they exceed .11, those in column *B* if they exceed .16 (p <.001, two-tailed, assuming a simple random sample).

Veterans and nonveterans differed little in their evaluations of past U.S. actions in Vietnam; both groups were split almost equally between those who tended toward support and those who tended to be critical. But in their feelings about amnesty, the groups differed noticeably. While 36 percent of the nonveterans agreed or agreed mostly that the men who went to Canada to avoid fighting in Vietnam were doing what they felt was right and should not be punished, only 18 percent of the veterans agreed or agreed mostly. In answer to the comparison question stating that going to Canada was wrong and those who did so should be punished, 78 percent of the veterans agreed or agreed mostly, compared to 61 percent of the nonveterans. It is perhaps understandable that most civilians who once served in the armed forces themselves would have little tolerance for those who avoided service by going to Canada.

One other difference is worth noting between veterans and nonveterans. The veterans showed greater support for the idea of career men in the military rather than citizen-soldiers, whereas the opposite was true for nonveterans. The data are summarized in table 7.

Table 8 displays two questions which deal with veterans' reactions to their military service and their perceptions of family reactions. Most veterans reported their own feelings as positive; nevertheless, there was room for variation. This variation in feeling about one's own military experience is strongly associated with other attitudes about military matters. Perceptions about family reactions were more balanced between positive and negative views. The two items shown in table 8 were only modestly correlated (r=.23). This finding, coupled with the different levels of positive feeling shown in the two items, indicates that some veterans held positive feelings about their military experience in spite of a perception that their entry into the service was not especially favored by family members.

Veterans' own feelings about having served are strongly correlated with feelings about the possibility of a son's enlistment (r=.53). These feelings about having served are

TABLE 7

Preference for Citizen-Soldiers versus Career Men

Scores on the Index	Veterans (N=324)	Nonveterans (N=385)
1.0-2.0 Prefer career men	46%	31%
2.5 Mixed feelings	24	26
3.0-4.0 Prefer citizen-soldiers	30	43
Total	100	100

TABLE 8

Veterans' Feelings about Having Served

Would you say your feelings about having been in the military are:

1. Strongly positive	38%
2. Mostly positive	43
3. Mostly negative	14
4. Strongly negative	5
Total	100

Which of the following best describes the feelings of your family when they first learned you were going to enter the service?

1. They were very much in favor of it	20%
2. Somewhat in favor	26
3. Neutral or indifferent	25
4. Somewhat dissatisfied	22
5. Very much dissatisfied	8
Total	101

also related to a number of other dimensions, as shown in column *B* of table 6. The pattern of correlations is similar to the factor loadings shown in table 3; those items which are most positively or negatively associated with a general factor of promilitary sentiment are also most strongly linked to veterans' feelings about their own military experience.

In column *B* of table 6, veterans' positive feelings about their military service are correlated with perceptions that the military organization offers fair treatment and competent leadership. Veterans with positive feelings about their past service were also likely to prefer fairly high levels of military influence, view the role of the military in our society as being predominantly positive, support past U.S. actions in Vietnam, show above average opposition to amnesty, and state that servicemen should obey orders without question.

We explored several other dimensions of veterans' experiences to see if they correlated with our measures of military attitudes. No substantial or consistent differences were found to be associated with branch of service (Army, Navy, Air Force, Marines). There also appeared to be no clear differences in attitudes between those veterans who had been drafted and those who had enlisted, although most of the veterans who had enlisted thought they would have been drafted otherwise.

One dimension which did show some consistent differences is length of past military service. Most of our civilian respondents who served in the military remained in the service no more than four years. But those who had served longer tended to show attitudes more favorable to the military. In particular, the greater the length of service among these veterans, the higher their ratings of fair treatment and competent leadership in the military. These findings are probably a reflection of career orientation among the longer-serving veterans.

In summary, the effect of personal contact with the military was not found to be as strong as is sometimes supposed. This might well indicate the differences between studies of large and representative samples as opposed to those focusing on case studies of individuals or organized groups such as the VFW or VVAW (see Helmer, 1974). There was, of course, enormous variation in attitudes within the group of veterans, as was true for the nonveterans as well. Some of this variation among veterans can be explained in terms of differing evaluations of their own military experience. However, a recent study of personal contact with governmental agencies (see Katz et al., 1975) found that only *negatively* evaluated contact has any effect different from no contact at all. Similarly we found consistent relationships between the evaluation of military experience and military attitudes but little relationship between veteran status and attitudes. Most veterans were positive in their evaluation, as shown in table 8. So it appears that those with negative contact were negative in their views, but those with positive contact did not have greatly different scores from those with no contact. Had the evaluations of past military service been more evenly distributed, the lack of differences in mean scores between veterans and nonveterans could have resulted from an averaging process, but that was not the case here. Those who had negative experiences also had negative attitudes; those who had positive experiences looked like those with none at all, i.e., like nonveterans.

Summary and Conclusion

In this look at the public view of the military, we have stressed several different themes.

First, we noted a fairly strong pattern of intercorrelations among the different dimensions along which people rated the military and its mission. In general, we found that those who were most favorable toward the military along one dimension tended to be among the more favorable—or less critical—along other dimensions. They were also more likely to have positive feelings about the possibility of a son's enlistment.

The second finding, that the military and its mission received "mixed reviews" at the hands of a national cross section of civilians, may help shed light on some apparently discrepant prior research findings. As we reported in the previous chapter, several studies found that the public rejected Vietnam policy to an increasing degree during the late sixties and early seventies, but other research indicated that the public fairly consistently gave high ratings to military leaders and to the job that the military was doing for the country. We have argued that these two kinds of findings are not incompatible, particularly if the government, rather than the military leadership, was blamed for involving the U.S. in Vietnam. At the same time, it must be acknowledged that those most strongly critical of Vietnam policy also tended to be the least supportive of the military along other dimensions, thus suggesting that for some individuals a frustration with Vietnam policy may have led to a heightened dissatisfaction with the military as a whole.

Evaluations of the military and its mission vary somewhat across different groups. Younger college graduates as a group not only called the use of military force into question, but were also critical of virtually all aspects of the military organization and existing civil-military relations. Older nongraduates as a group, however, showed predominantly promilitary attitudes, but were still critical of the use of military force for intervention, high levels of military spending, and the fairness of treatment within the military. When we compared veterans and nonveterans, we found few differences in attitudes about the military. The veterans were, however, more likely to rate the military as less influential, were more strongly opposed to amnesty, and were more supportive of a career military than were nonveterans. Within the group of veterans there were variations in ratings of the military, i.e., those who were dissatisfied with their own service experience tended to be less favorable to the military as a whole.

4
Military Men View the Military

Homogeneity and Diversity among Military Men

The beliefs of military men, as reflected in most of the literature on the military mind, have been seen as being quite homogeneous. Abrahamsson (1972) has indicated that there are four homogenization processes among the professional military. They are: (1) self-selection through initial interest or motivation; (2) screening procedures used by the military; (3) continuous selection and retention within the profession; and (4) professional socialization and training.

For the purposes of this study, we will assume that all the processes may be operating. The literature emphasizes the processes of self-selection (Lovell, 1964) or anticipatory socialization (Lucas, 1971) as the primary mechanisms. Socialization effects have been difficult to demonstrate (cf. French and Ernest, 1955; Campbell and McCormack, 1957; Roghmann and Sodeur, 1972). Lovell (1964), in his study of West Point cadets, does show that there is growing homogeneity in attitudes over a period of time which supports the arguments presented here. However, the impact of socialization on direction of attitude change as revealed by his data is modest. It should also be noted that Abrahamsson (1972) is explicitly dealing with *professional* military men, and all four processes are more likely to be at work (and over a longer period) than would be indicated in relatively short-term studies of a cross section of draftees or officer candidates.

This literature, then, reflects a general emphasis on the professional military, not on the military as a whole. There has been a tendency to define the military as consisting of high-level, professional officers (see Mills, 1956; Huntington, 1957, 1963; Janowitz, 1960; Keller, 1963; Monsen and Cannon, 1965; Domhoff, 1967; Russett, 1974). This emphasis on the study of military elites has led to an overemphasis on the processes of homogenization, thus overlooking important differences among subgroups within the uniformed military. In this chapter we will focus on those subgroup differences.

In a sense, we are dealing with the question: who is the most "military"? This question can be examined by looking at the nature of both vertical and horizontal differences within the military. The vertical dimension consists of rank and may be treated as a dichotomy forming two status groups—officers and enlisted personnel. This distinction has been an important one historically (Stouffer et al., 1949), and each group has been studied separately (Janowitz, 1960; Moskos, 1970). Along this vertical dimension, officers are considered more professional and, thus, more "military" than enlisted men.[1] A further distinction can be made within each of these status groups: the higher the rank, the more professional, i.e., the more the homogenization processes have been at work.

Horizontally, there are major differences as well. The most fundamental of these, and of increasing importance during the Vietnam era (Moskos, 1970, 1973b; Helmer, 1974; Cortwright, 1975), is the distinction between career

---

1. We recognize that there is potential disagreement over whether the officer corps truly constitutes a profession in the sense that medicine and law are professions. This controversy aside, there remain major differences between officers and enlisted personnel in terms of education, commitment, career patterns, and responsibilities that might lead one to expect officers to be more "military" in the aggregate than enlisted personnel, and senior noncommissioned officers more "military" than junior enlisted grades.

men ("lifers") and noncareer men (see also Karsten, 1971; Van Doorn, 1976.)[2] Concern has also been expressed about a separate military ethos resulting from the elimination, or at least reduction, of the noncareer group in an all-volunteer force (Janowitz, 1971, 1973; Johnston and Bachman, 1972; Moskos, 1973a; Bachman and Blair, 1975). We have discussed this general problem at length in chapter 1.

Other possible subgroup differences are those between services and between branches within the services, with the emphasis being on how traditional the military service or branch is, e.g., the combat arms can be seen as "more military" than service support branches.

Selection of Analysis Groups within the Military

Our examination of the literature suggested that the primary vertical and horizontal distinctions outlined above should be the focus for our analysis. Accordingly, officers were contrasted with enlisted men, and career-oriented men were compared to those who did not plan military careers. As a result, the belief systems of four basic groups were examined: career officers, career enlisted men, noncareer officers, and noncareer enlisted men. We use the term "belief system" in this context to refer to an interrelated set of values, preferences, and perceptions about the military and its mission.

Any attempt to dichotomize military men into those who are and are not career oriented must be somewhat arbitrary. In the present analysis we have treated as career oriented those who expected to reenlist and make the military a career, plus those who planned to reenlist but were undecided about a military career. The small number who expected to retire at the end of their tour of duty were also considered to be career men. We have treated as noncareer

2. Although we have treated them as conceptually distinct, rank and career orientation are empirically related in our sample, i.e., a higher proportion of officers than of enlisted men are career oriented.

oriented those who planned not to reenlist, plus those who expected to reenlist but did not intend to make the military a career.

Before we decided on the present form of analysis, we carried out extensive analyses of the 1972–73 Navy data. These analyses included comparisons between first-term enlisted men who planned to reenlist and those who did not. The differences between these two groups of first termers were substantial, and essentially the same as the more general career/noncareer differences presented later in this chapter. On the whole, our analyses of the 1972–73 Navy data (Bachman, 1974; Blair, 1975; Bachman and Blair, 1976) confirmed our basic expectations: career men were consistently different from noncareer men. We also found some differences between officers and enlisted men, but these were not as strong or as consistent as those based on career orientation. Many of these 1972–73 analyses are presented below in combination with recent ones using the 1974–75 sample of Army respondents.

Hypothesized Changes from 1972–73 to 1974–75

Prior to examining the Army data we developed several hypotheses about the differences or similarities we expected to find between the Army and the Navy data. These hypotheses did not deal with any presumed differences between the two branches of service (Army versus Navy). Rather, our hypotheses were based on assumptions about the conditions in 1974–75 as compared with those in 1972–73.

With respect to issues of self-selection in an all-volunteer context, our expectations were quite straightforward. Without draft motivation, we hypothesized that processes of ideological self-selection would become more important. Accordingly, we expected that more favorable beliefs about the military would be required for noncareer men to enter voluntarily than had been true for noncareer men under pressures of conscription. Hence, we expected the noncareer men in the Army sample to be somewhat more promilitary than their counterparts in the Navy sample had been. Career Army men, however, were not expected to be much different from their Navy counterparts. Such men had (by definition) self-selected to stay in the military, and the historical change from conscription to voluntarism was not expected to be of consequence to the favorableness of their beliefs about the military. For these reasons, we expected that the ideological gap between career men and noncareer men would be reduced. However, we did not expect the gap to be entirely eliminated since noncareer men (by definition) do not have long-term commitments even if they are willing to serve voluntarily for a time.

One further expectation should be noted. We considered it likely that the proportion of servicemen who were career oriented would be higher under all-volunteer conditions than it was under conscription conditions.

Thus, prior to examination of the Army data, our hypotheses were—

1. Noncareer men in the Army (1974–75) would be more promilitary than their Navy (1972–73) counterparts, since the Army men were serving voluntarily rather than under conditions of actual conscription or draft-motivated enlistment.
2. Career Army men would not be appreciably different from their Navy counterparts (both would be very promilitary).
3. As a result of hypotheses 1 and 2, the consistent ideological differences found between noncareer and career men (for both officers and enlisted men) in the 1972–73 Navy sample would be smaller in the 1974–75 Army sample.
4. The proportion of total military personnel who are career oriented would be greater in the Army sample than in the Navy sample.
5. As a result of hypotheses 1 and 4, the ideological differences between military men and civilians would increase (*a*) because Army noncareer men could be

expected to be somewhat less ideologically representative of civilians than were Navy noncareer men and
(*b*) because the proportion of those who were career
oriented, and hence unrepresentative of their civilian counterparts, was expected to increase.

Before we turn to our analysis of differences in beliefs
based on rank and career orientation, a reminder of our
overall plan of analysis may be in order. In this chapter, we
will examine the nature of the "ideological" cleavages *within
the military*. We will *not* make any comparisons between civilians and military men. Chapter 5 and much of chapter 6
will be devoted to comparing civilians with military men.

Diversity among Military Men by
Career Orientation and Rank

As our first step in examining the nature of military men's
belief systems, we will present an illustrative analysis similar
to the one we presented for civilians by age and education
in chapter 3. For simplicity of presentation and comparison,
we have dichotomized the many possible rank groups into
two sample groups, officers and enlisted men. In addition,
we have separated our samples into those who were career
oriented and those who were not.

Throughout this chapter we will be using the first of
the sixteen basic measures, the index of perceived military
job opportunity, in order to illustrate a series of points and
to introduce the groups that we have compared. In figure 3
we have presented this measure related to career orientation and to rank. Both Army and Navy groups show clear
differences according to the respondents' career orientation. The Army data in the figure show some differences by
rank as well.

Enlisted Men: Career and Noncareer

In figure 4 we have contrasted the mean scores of both
career and noncareer Army and Navy enlisted groups with

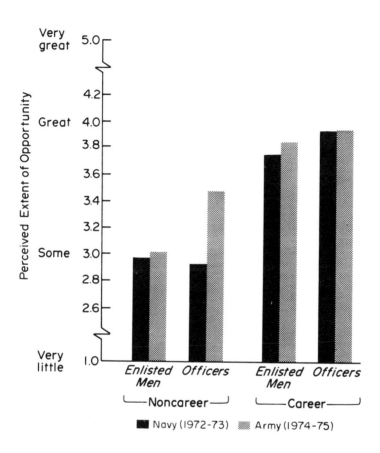

Fig. 3. Military job opportunity index related to career orientation and rank. The data used to construct this figure are presented in tables 18 and 19 in Appendix D.

the substantive midpoint or neutral point of each measure (using the same data display technique we employed in our analysis of civilians). The middle line represents this neutral point—midway between those responses that we have termed antimilitary and those we have designated as promilitary. The mean scores, then, are plotted in terms of standard deviation units based on their relationship to the midpoint.[3]

The mean ratings by noncareer enlisted men were fairly close to the neutral point along many of our sixteen dimensions. Their strongest criticism was directed at unfair treatment within the military service. They also gave military leaders rather low competency ratings, and they did not agree with the idea of unquestioning military obedience. These noncareer enlisted men were not very supportive of military intervention to aid other countries, nor were they positive about past U.S. actions in Vietnam. However, they were somewhat supportive of the maintenance of U.S. military supremacy.

Evaluation of civil-military relations by noncareer enlisted men was mixed. The current level of military spending was seen to be appropriate; the role of the military in society was viewed as neither negative nor positive; military (versus civilian) influence was perceived to be generally in balance, although more than the present level of military influence was preferred and thus, overall, military influence was seen as inadequate. This latter finding was stronger in

---

3. The actual mean scores for figure 4 (and also figure 5) can be found in Appendix D. Generally, a difference between the two enlisted groups (either Army or Navy) of more than .09 or .15 standard deviation units is statistically significant at the $p < .05$ or $p < .001$ level (two-tailed) respectively. (The standard significance tests have been developed for strict random samples, whereas the military and civilian samples used in the present study are based on multistage stratified probability sampling with some degree of clustering. There exist some rather complex methods for estimating significance levels with such samples. However, for our present purposes it will be adequate to use the significance tests for random samples, particularly if we rely on the more stringent .001 criterion rather than the usual .05 level.)

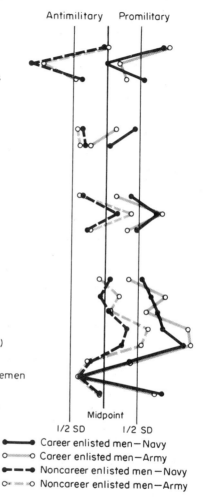

The Military Organization
  Perceived military job opportunities
  Perceived fair treatment in services
  Perceived competence of military leaders

Military Obedience
  Servicemen should obey without question
  Should obey in My Lai-type situation

Foreign Policy and Use of Force
  Support for military intervention
  Preference for U.S. military supremacy
  Support for U.S. actions in Vietnam

Civil-Military Relations
  Role of military seen as positive
  Preference for higher military spending
  Perceived military (vs. civilian) influence
  Preferred military (vs. civilian) influence
  Adequacy of military influence (perc.—pref.)
  Preference for citizen-soldiers
  Preferred wide range of views among servicemen
  Support for amnesty

Antimilitary   Promilitary

Midpoint
1/2 SD   1/2 SD
●——————● Career enlisted men—Navy
○═════○ Career enlisted men—Army
●— — —● Noncareer enlisted men—Navy
○═ ═ ═○ Noncareer enlisted men—Army

Fig. 4. Comparison of career and noncareer enlisted groups. The data used to construct this figure are presented in tables 16 and 18 in Appendix D.

the Army sample. In spite of this preference for somewhat greater military influence, the noncareer enlisted men tended to prefer citizen-soldiers over career men and supported a wide range of political views among servicemen.

By way of contrast, the mean ratings by career enlisted men were on the promilitary side of nearly every measure. They had more mixed views on the fairness of treatment in the services and on what soldiers should do in a My Lai situation. They were strongly promilitary on issues of civil-military relations, especially in their views of civil-military influence.

The most basic finding shown in the figure is that those enlisted men with career commitments were strongly and consistently more favorable to the military than those enlisted men who expected to be leaving the service. Thus, both in an absolute sense (compared to the neutral point on the scale) and in a relative sense (compared to noncareer men), career-oriented enlisted men were quite promilitary in their views. The next question is whether these career/ noncareer differences appeared among officers as well.

Officers: Career and Noncareer

Figure 5 presents a comparison of the views of career and noncareer officers. For the Navy, the same pattern of relative differences found among career/noncareer enlisted men is found among officers: career officers were generally more promilitary than noncareer officers.[4]

In the aggregate, career officers (in both Army and Navy samples) showed a great consistency in promilitary responses, except for the issues of obedience in My Lai and the range of political views among servicemen. In particular, they saw job opportunities in the military as very good, the competence of military leaders as very high, and the role of

_____

4. Generally, a difference between the two officer groups of more than .25 or .42 standard deviation units for the Navy, and .32 or .54 for the Army, is statistically significant at the $p < .05$ or $p < .001$ level (two-tailed) respectively.

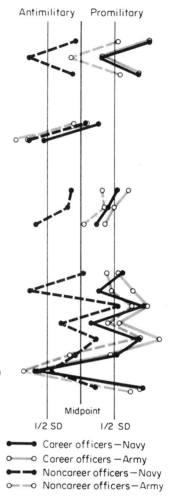

The Military Organization
  Perceived military job opportunities
  Perceived fair treatment in services
  Perceived competence of military leaders

Military Obedience
  Servicemen should obey without question
  Should obey in My Lai-type situation

Foreign Policy and Use of Force
  Support for military intervention
  Preference for U.S. military supremacy
  Support for U.S. actions in Vietnam

Civil-Military Relations
  Role of military seen as positive
  Preference for higher military spending
  Perceived military (vs. civilian) influence
  Preferred military (vs. civilian) influence
  Adequacy of military influence (perc.—pref.)
  Preference for citizen-soldiers
  Preferred wide range of views among servicemen
  Support for amnesty

Antimilitary   Promilitary

Midpoint
1/2 SD   1/2 SD

●━━━● Career officers—Navy
○┄┄┄○ Career officers—Army
●━ ━● Noncareer officers—Navy
○┄ ┄○ Noncareer officers—Army

Fig. 5. Comparison of career and noncareer officer groups. The data used to construct this figure are presented in tables 16 and 19 in Appendix D.

military in society as very positive. Furthermore, they noted military influence as very low, amnesty as unacceptable, military intervention as potentially necessary, and career men as preferable to citizen-soldiers. Army career officers were especially supportive of U.S. military supremacy and even more likely to see military influence as inadequate.

Noncareer Navy officers, like noncareer enlisted men, gave the military mixed ratings. Here, the most consistent set of findings dealt with the use of military force. There was little support for military intervention and for U.S. military supremacy. Also, there was a good deal of criticism of U.S. policy in Vietnam. The evaluations of the military organization were either neutral (on the average) or negative. The noncareer Navy officers were, like noncareer enlisted men, critical of unfair treatment in the military. Military job opportunities were not seen as very great, nor were leaders given high ratings.

Noncareer Navy officers' attitudes about civil-military relations were partly positive and partly negative. They evaluated the role of the military in society as somewhere between positive and negative. They saw the military budget as excessive. They perceived the military as having *very* low levels of influence vis-à-vis civilians, while their preferences were for only *moderately* low levels of military influence.

The noncareer officer group was the one category for which the Army data did not closely replicate the Navy findings. Whereas the Navy noncareer officers in 1972–73 had mixed evaluations of the military, the Army noncareer officers in 1974–75 were, in most respects, promilitary in their beliefs. Thus the Army *noncareer* officers were not very different from *career* officers in both the Army and the Navy.

Differences between the Navy (1972–73) and the Army (1974–75)

On the whole, the Army data, although collected two years later (after the implementation of the all-volunteer force), replicated the findings for the Navy remarkably well. For three of the four major analysis groups, the mean scores on the sixteen measures are nearly identical. The one area of substantive difference concerns the adequacy of military (versus civilian) influence. Army men from all four groups wanted to see *more* military influence than did their counterparts in the Navy.

The fourth analysis group, noncareer officers, shows some important Army-Navy differences. Navy junior officers without career commitments were quite similar to noncareer enlisted men. Army junior officers without career commitments appeared to be much more like career officers. We had anticipated that an Army replication of the Navy data would reveal that the gap between career and noncareer men—both officers and enlisted men—had grown somewhat smaller. Instead, we found essentially no change in the size of the career/noncareer differences among *enlisted men*, whereas the differences among *officers* had almost disappeared.

Why were the findings for the Army data different than we had hypothesized? At this point we can only speculate on why they were different and present an admittedly ex post facto explanation. Our interpretation still focuses on issues of self-selection as did our initial hypotheses. However, it has become increasingly clearer that conceptualizations of the nature and consequences of self-selection among both officers and enlisted men must be more differentiated than we had originally anticipated.

The consequences of draft conditions may have been overestimated for most enlisted men. Military service performs certain social functions for many young men, the same as attending institutions of higher learning does for their nonmilitary age peers. In particular, military service provides an opportunity for leaving home and developing higher levels of autonomy and financial independence. It may be that most young, noncareer men are joining the Army for other reasons than wanting to be a soldier and that, furthermore, young men in the past also joined for those reasons (although they may have justified their service in terms of actual conscription or draft motivation). The views which these noncareer enlisted men express about the military may reflect either the attitudes of their civilian age and educational counterparts (whom they match quite closely as will be shown in chapter 5) or high levels of disappointment with the military organization they have volunteered to join, or a combination of both. Our own guess is that there is relatively little ideological self-selection among enlisted men who do not have apparent career commitments to the military. Thus they are essentially representative of their civilian peers in their levels of pro- or antimilitary sentiment.

For noncareer officers the self-selection process (under all-volunteer conditions) may work quite differently. First it should be noted that the *level* of self-selection and the *length of time* it must be sustained must be greater among officers. To be an officer, one must volunteer long before one enters service (which is in sharp contrast to the situation for most enlisted men who may find themselves in the military quite quickly after visiting the recruiter and volunteering). During this long time span prior to actual service, one could at any time drop out, e.g., after the first or second year of ROTC. A greater commitment to the military or, at a minimum, a greater acceptance of its legitimacy and purpose may well be required to sustain a potential officer during this period prior to accepting a commission and serving. In addition, the social functions concerned with growing up should not be as relevant for potential officers who already have that chance in institutions of higher learning. Finally, college graduates are likely to have a wider range of other options open to them than nongraduates. Thus college graduates who join as officers probably have to be more ideologically self-selected than the typical volunteer for the enlisted ranks.

However, there is also the possibility that our Army data underestimated the differences between career and noncareer officers because of historical conditions unique to the Army at this time. Our measure of career orientation required only an indication on the part of the respondent that he planned to stay in the Army. In studing the Navy we felt that it was a conservative measure. If we could find substantial differences between career and noncareer men using only this definition of career orientation, then there were surely considerable differences in fact. In the case of the Army, however, the situation is more complex. It is possible that some proportion of the Army officers who indicated that they would be leaving the Army were, at one time, very career oriented, but at the time of survey, were expecting to leave because of reductions in force. This condition, if true, should apply primarily to noncareer Army captains who came in during the Vietnam War, stayed on, and (as of 1974–75) expected to be forced to leave or felt that job opportunities were lacking. (There were only a few cases in the data set of more senior officers who were leaving.) Therefore, in examining the Army data in more detail later in this chapter, we always distinguish between lieutenants and captains among both career and noncareer officer groups. For the Navy junior officers this was not a potential problem; they were examined as a group (including ensigns, lieutenants junior grade, and lieutenants).

Our findings, with those exceptions noted above, are clearly consistent with our expectations based on the literature. There are important cleavages by rank, and still larger differences according to career orientation. But there are alternative approaches to the data which could, perhaps more accurately, "explain" ideological diversity among military men.

Sources of Variation:
Individual or Organizational Characteristics?

The original analyses of the Navy data focused primarily on age and to some extent on education as the primary sources of variation among military men as well as among civilians. Strong relationships were found between the age of the

Navy men and the various measures under consideration (see Bachman, 1973). In addition, education was also found to be an important source of differences in beliefs about the military (Bachman, 1973, 1974; Bowers and Bachman, 1974). The arguments presented above, however, focus on organizational characteristics such as career orientation and rank, rather than on individual characteristics such as age and education. The problem is complicated because age and career orientation are highly interrelated, as are education and rank. Most younger men in both the Navy and the Army were not career oriented and were planning to leave; most older men in the military were career oriented and were staying. In addition, most officers were college graduates; most enlisted men were not.

Blair (1975) presented the age and education distributions for the four Navy career and rank groups we have been considering. The same relationships were found for the four Army groups. Age is clearly related to career orientation; education is equally related to rank. We have also analyzed race, region, urbanicity, and parental education distributions for the four groups in each sample.

There are some differences in the distributions among the four groups. For example, career men were more likely to come from rural areas and small towns and to have less educated parents than their noncareer counterparts. There are smaller proportions of blacks among officers than among enlisted men. These particular differences, however, are not large and could not account for the many substantial differences we found between those who were career oriented and those who were not (nor could they account for other smaller differences).

But the differences between career groups in age distributions and the discrepancies between rank groups in education might provide alternative explanations for the findings presented above. Blair (1975) presented a detailed examination of both those variables we have termed organizational characteristics and those we have called individual characteristics in an attempt to sort out alternative explanations for the diversity in belief systems of military men. Several aspects of those analyses should be noted:

1. Race, region and community of origin, and parental education *alone* generally do not have much relative predictive power compared to age and education or career orientation and rank.

2. Organizational characteristics of the respondent as reflected by his rank and career orientation seem to be the best overall predictors and match or exceed the predictive power of the two most powerful individual predictors, age and education.

3. However, it should also be noted that there is a great overlap between individual characteristics and organizational characteristics of the respondents.

4. Parallel analyses for the Army data showed the same kinds of relationships. Once again, organizational characteristics were found to be the best overall predictors of beliefs concerning the military.

5. Interestingly, however, other organizational characteristics which we had anticipated would predict military ideology among Army men failed to show any independent contribution to the explanation of the variance in the measures. Whether or not an Army man was in the combat arms showed no independent effects once career orientation and rank were controlled. The same is true for kinds of combat experience in Vietnam or the number of tours in Vietnam.

Blair (1975) demonstrated how age operates primarily as a proxy for career orientation, i.e., how age appears to be the source of variation (or determinant or cause of differences) when, in reality, the primary source of differences in beliefs among military men is their career orientation or lack of it. The reader should keep in mind that the statistical relationships we find between age and the sixteen measures of military views are not spurious; but it would be erroneous to *interpret* the relationships in terms of differences in age leading to differences in beliefs rather than in terms of differences in career orientation as the primary link to diversity in beliefs.

In addition to the statistical manipulations which have shown age to be a proxy variable, there is another approach to this question. If age and education (individual characteristics) were really more important in predicting ideology among military men than are their rank and career orientation (organizational characteristics), then we should be able to predict the attitudes of military groups based on the beliefs of civilians who are their counterparts in age and education. Generally, age has the same relationship to the measures we are examining among civilians as it does among military men, but it is much weaker among civilians. Education, on the other hand, relates to the military views of civilians quite differently than in the case of military men. Specifically, better educated civilians were consistently more antimilitary, whereas better educated military men (officers) were either more promilitary or else the differences were very small. Most importantly, when we compare career men to their civilian age and educational counterparts, they are consistently and substantially different. (The same finding applies to noncareer Army officers as well.)

Organizational Characteristics and Diversity among Military Men

Diversity among Enlisted Men

Returning to the example of perceived military job opportunities, we see again the distinctions between those who were career oriented and those who were not (fig. 6). In addition there are some differences among career men which could reflect greater military professionalism, i.e., the senior noncommissioned officers (NCO's) were more promilitary than were career-oriented, but more junior, enlisted men or NCO's. Once again, one must not forget that

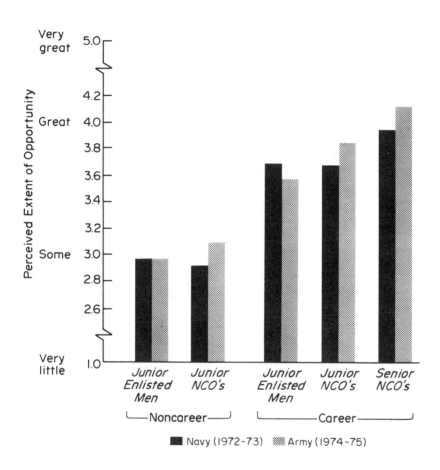

Fig. 6. Military job opportunity index related to career and noncareer enlisted groups.

the most substantial and most consistent differences lie between those men who were and those who were not career oriented.[5]

In tables 9 and 10 we have detailed information for five enlisted groups in each military sample. For over one-half of the measures there are not only the career/noncareer differences found in *all* of them, but also differences by "stage in career" or level of rank among career men. The senior NCO's were more promilitary than younger career-oriented enlisted men, in terms of their perceptions of military job opportunities, perceptions of fair treatment, perceptions of military (versus civilian) influence, and perceptions of adequacy of influence. Furthermore, they were more promilitary in their support for military intervention, support for U.S. action in Vietnam, opposition to amnesty, support for unquestioning military obedience, and support for obedience in a My Lai-type situation.

At the other end of the continuum, noncareer junior enlisted men were even more antimilitary than noncareer junior NCO's along some dimensions, such as perceptions about military (versus civilian) influence, support for military intervention, and amnesty.

In summary, we have seen that the primary source of diversity among enlisted men is based on career orientation. In addition, senior career enlisted men are more promilitary than junior career men, although that difference is neither universal nor as strong as the difference based on career orientation. Also, among the noncareer-oriented, junior enlisted men are generally somewhat more antimilitary than junior NCO's.

Diversity among Officers

Once again we return to a graphic example of the variations we are examining. In figure 7 we display the mean scores of

---

5. For purposes of this analysis, junior enlisted men are those in grades E–1 through E–4, junior NCO's are those in grades E–5 and E–6, and senior NCO's are those in grades E–7 through E–9.

TABLE 9

Mean Scores for Navy Career and Noncareer Enlisted Groups

	Noncareer			Career	
	Junior Enlisted Men (N=876)	Junior NCO's (N=235)	Junior Enlisted Men (N=191)	Junior NCO's (N=408)	Senior NCO's (N=273)
The Military Organization					
Perceived military job opportunities	2.97	2.92	3.68	3.67	3.95
Perceived fair treatment in services	1.96	1.96	2.85	2.93	3.20
Perceived competence of military leaders	2.62	2.73	3.30	3.42	3.76
Military Obedience					
Servicemen should obey without question	2.13	2.31	2.68	2.96	3.06
Should obey in My Lai-type situation	1.81	1.63	2.09	2.06	1.94
Foreign Policy and Use of Force					
Support for military intervention	2.19	2.43	2.58	2.80	2.98
Preference for U.S. military supremacy	2.69	2.61	3.17	3.19	3.24
Support for U.S. actions in Vietnam	2.32	2.31	2.71	2.84	2.94
Civil-Military Relations					
Role of military seen as positive	2.54	2.55	2.87	2.88	2.84
Preference for higher military spending	2.95	3.03	3.49	3.73	3.53
Perceived military (vs. civilian) influence	3.08	2.42	2.79	2.07	1.82
Preferred military (vs. civilian) influence	3.30	3.27	3.74	3.77	3.60
Adequacy of military influence (perc.−pref.)	3.79	3.16	3.05	2.30	2.22
Preference for citizen-soldiers	2.69	2.43	2.44	2.11	2.04
Preferred wide range of views among servicemen	2.74	2.91	2.79	2.75	2.71
Support for amnesty	2.66	2.11	2.09	1.44	1.25

TABLE 10

Mean Scores for Army Career and Noncareer Enlisted Groups

	Noncareer			Career	
	Junior Enlisted Men (N=704)	Junior NCO's (N=175)	Junior Enlisted Men (N=255)	Junior NCO's (N=449)	Senior NCO's (N=225)
The Military Organization					
Perceived military job opportunities	2.97	3.08	3.58	3.84	4.13
Perceived fair treatment in services	2.12	2.20	2.84	3.18	3.41
Perceived competence of military leaders	2.53	2.59	3.10	3.23	3.58
Military Obedience					
Servicemen should obey without question	2.04	2.17	2.59	2.73	2.71
Should obey in My Lai-type situation	1.73	1.64	1.93	1.81	1.77
Foreign Policy and Use of Force					
Support for military intervention	2.15	2.39	2.41	2.65	2.85
Preference for U.S. military supremacy	2.82	2.94	3.09	3.30	3.41
Support for U.S. actions in Vietnam	2.33	2.40	2.63	2.76	2.84
Civil-Military Relations					
Role of military seen as positive	2.46	2.55	2.69	2.77	2.81
Preference for higher military spending	3.16	3.30	3.69	3.88	3.95
Perceived military (vs. civilian) influence	3.02	2.39	3.00	2.17	1.89
Preferred military (vs. civilian) influence	3.51	3.70	3.95	4.09	4.04
Adequacy of military influence (perc.−pref.)	3.50	2.69	3.05	2.08	1.85
Preference for citizen-soldiers	2.77	2.48	2.43	2.05	1.99
Preferred wide range of views among servicemen	2.78	2.95	2.73	2.75	2.71
Support for amnesty	2.67	1.96	2.17	1.56	1.29

five groups of Navy officers and six groups of Army officers on the index of perceived military job opportunities. We must note immediately that only nineteen of the more senior Navy officers were not career oriented. They have proven to be an interesting group, but the reader must remember that the small sample size may not provide very accurate estimates of the attitudes of officers in this category. However, the findings are consistent with our expectations that these were, presumably, once career-oriented officers who became disillusioned with the Navy (or, alternatively, the Navy with them). This is quite different from the expectations we held for noncareer Army captains who, presumably, were being forced out to reduce the size of the Army. (The sample sizes are also small for several Army groups.)[6]

In figure 7 the career/noncareer distinction remains solid for Navy officers. The senior officers who were leaving the Navy were most antimilitary and may have reflected the disillusionment mentioned above. Such disillusionment, for example, may have been rooted in the experience of the Vietnam War, or with the changes imposed on the "old Navy" by Admiral Elmo Zumwalt in bringing the service into the all-volunteer era. That is, their disillusionment might have been with the Navy generally, or only with the "new Navy." Other senior officers and warrant officers (who were also older) were the most promilitary.

Among Army officers, some career/noncareer differences are evident in figure 7, but the differences are considerably smaller than those found for the Navy. The figure shows basically no differences between noncareer lieutenants and captains in their perceptions of military job opportunities.

In table 11 the mean scores for the five Navy officer groups are presented. For Navy officers, career/noncareer differences are consistent with the pattern illustrated in

6. For purposes of this analysis, junior officers are those in grades 0–1 through 0–3, and senior officers are those in grades 0–4 and above.

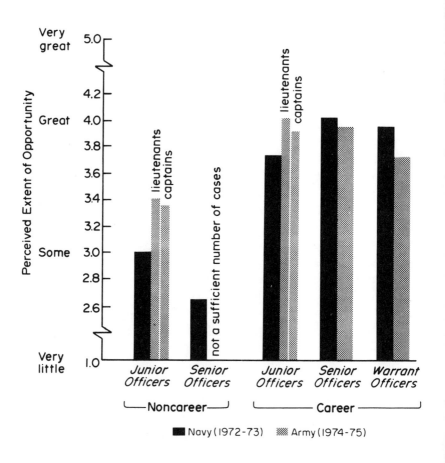

Fig. 7. Military job opportunity index related to career and noncareer
        officer groups.

figure 7. Generally, the most antimilitary group consisted of the senior officers who were leaving the Navy. Warrant officers and senior commissioned officers expecting to remain in service were the most promilitary. However, the main finding of table 11 reinforces our conclusion that it was career orientation that made the primary difference among Navy officers, just as it did among enlisted men (both Army and Navy).

The pattern of weaker career/noncareer differences among Army officers is reflected in table 12. There were also only modest differences between noncareer lieutenants (the least career-oriented group) and noncareer captains (a group that may have been career oriented at one time as indicated above). Hence, even the group of Army officers (noncareer lieutenants) most likely to parallel the junior noncareer officers in the Navy was still quite similar in ideology to the career officer groups (both Army and Navy).

Attitude Change or Self-selection?

The findings reported throughout this chapter are consistent in showing strong career/noncareer differences in the ideologies of military men. In the next chapter we will see that career men were different not only from noncareer servicemen, but from their civilian age and educational counterparts as well. In our discussion of the findings to this point, we have stressed the importance of self-selection as the probable cause of these differences. But that is not the only possible explanation.

We noted at the beginning of this chapter that first-term enlisted men showed rather different sets of beliefs about the military depending upon whether they did or did not plan to reenlist. Those first termers who planned to reenlist were much more promilitary and were very similar in ideology to later-term enlisted men (Bachman and Blair, 1976). We can distinguish two quite different explanations for this pattern of findings.

TABLE 11

Mean Scores for Navy Career and Noncareer Officer Groups

	Noncareer		Career		
	Junior Officers (N=66)	Senior Officers (N=19)	Junior Officers (N=80)	Senior Officers (N=110)	Warrant Officers (N=32)
The Military Organization					
Perceived military job opportunities	3.00	2.65	3.73	4.03	3.96
Perceived fair treatment in services	2.39	2.15	3.04	3.39	3.36
Perceived competence of military leaders	2.96	2.63	3.59	3.97	3.88
Military Obedience					
Servicemen should obey without question	2.60	2.56	2.73	2.78	2.81
Should obey in My Lai-type situation	1.46	1.37	1.59	1.53	1.84
Foreign Policy and Use of Force					
Support for military intervention	2.43	2.29	2.87	2.95	3.03
Preference for U.S. military supremacy	2.31	2.34	2.77	2.87	3.13
Support for U.S. actions in Vietnam	2.04	1.88	2.49	2.74	2.99
Civil-Military Relations					
Role of military seen as positive	2.57	2.37	2.90	2.99	2.82
Preference for higher military spending	2.40	1.94	3.28	3.20	3.56
Perceived military (vs. civilian) influence	2.44	2.49	2.17	1.91	1.70
Preferred military (vs. civilian) influence	2.78	2.74	3.20	3.08	3.18
Adequacy of military influence (perc.−pref.)	3.66	3.76	2.97	2.83	2.52
Preference for citizen-soldiers	2.47	2.79	2.11	2.08	1.84
Preferred wide range of views among servicemen	3.27	3.39	3.04	3.14	2.89
Support for amnesty	2.22	2.24	1.73	1.30	1.11

TABLE 12

Mean Scores for Army Career and Noncareer Officer Groups

	Noncareer		Career			Warrant
	2d/1st Lieutenant (N=25)	Captain (N=12)	2d/1st Lieutenant (N=55)	Captain (N=55)	Senior (N=44)	(N=39)
The Military Organization						
Perceived military job opportunities	3.40	3.35	4.02	3.91	3.96	3.72
Perceived fair treatment in services	2.70	2.65	3.35	3.28	3.41	2.97
Perceived competence of military leaders	3.46	3.33	3.82	3.99	3.74	3.60
Military Obedience						
Servicemen should obey without question	2.36	2.42	2.73	2.56	2.50	2.69
Should obey in My Lai-type situation	1.36	1.25	1.31	1.11	1.16	1.51
Foreign Policy and Use of Force						
Support for military intervention	2.64	2.91	3.18	2.95	3.18	2.97
Preference for U.S. military supremacy	2.70	2.83	2.91	2.79	2.90	3.22
Support for U.S. actions in Vietnam	2.49	2.68	2.70	2.73	2.79	2.85
Civil-Military Relations						
Role of military seen as positive	2.72	2.83	2.89	2.87	2.84	2.77
Preference for higher military spending	3.32	3.42	3.86	3.66	3.57	3.77
Perceived military (vs. civilian) influence	2.33	2.02	2.01	1.92	2.01	1.72
Preferred military (vs. civilian) influence	3.30	3.52	3.56	3.43	3.32	3.71
Adequacy of military influence (perc.–pref.)	3.02	2.50	2.45	2.49	2.69	2.01
Preference for citizen-soldiers	2.68	2.67	2.06	1.96	2.40	2.04
Preferred wide range of views among servicemen	3.28	3.21	2.91	3.06	3.22	3.13
Support for amnesty	1.88	1.50	1.52	1.62	1.44	1.22

1. During the first tour of duty, those individuals most likely to reenlist may undergo *attitude changes* in a more promilitary direction. This may occur through a process of socialization as a result of exposure to the more experienced military men who tend to hold such views, or through exposure to positive experiences in the service, or both.
2. By the time some individuals reach their late teens, they may be more favorable than others in their view of military services and mission. These differences, which exist prior to enlistment, may be among the factors influencing the *self-selection process* involved in the decision to reenlist.

While the only really adquate test of these two competing explanations would involve a longitudinal design, we felt that we could gain some insights by looking separately at first-term enlisted men who had served about one year, those who had served two years, and those who had served three or four years. If self-selection accounts for the differences between the attitudes of the career military men and others, there should be consistent differences in attitudes between those who did and did not plan on reenlistment, i.e., the differences for those in their first year should be just as large on the average as the differences found for those in their second, third, or fourth years of service. If, however, the attitude change explanation is correct, we *might* expect to see smaller differences among those in their first year, provided we make the assumption that the process of attitude change requires more than a few months to be completed.

Our basic finding was that the differences between first termers who planned to reenlist, and those who did not, were evident quite early. Those who had served about one year showed differences just as large on the average as those who had served several years longer. This finding is fully consistent with the self-selection explanation—the view that reenlistment is heavily influenced by rather deeply rooted perceptions and ideology related to the military life-style and mission. The alternative explanation, based on attitude changes during the first tour of duty, is not ruled out entirely. Both explanations could be true to some degree. Indeed, given the fact that reenlistment intention in the third year of service is more strongly related to actual reenlistment than is reenlistment intention after one year, it may be that some socialization effects are masked as self-selection. But whatever the pattern of causation, our analyses in this area demonstrate that it does *not* require years and years of service experience for first-term enlisted men to develop the promilitary attitudes found among later termers. For those who planned to reenlist, the promilitary attitudes were evident as early as the first year of service.

Summary and Conclusions

Our examination of belief systems concerning the military found among military men has been based on representative samples of Navy and Army personnel. The Navy data were collected in late 1972 and early 1973 and the Army data in late 1974 and early 1975. In this chapter we have stressed several different themes.

First, there is a lack of a definitive promilitary stance among military men as a whole. Aggregate responses would mask the large amount of diversity among military men in terms of their beliefs.

Second, careful examination of the sources of variation in attitudes showed that although age acts as a proxy variable for it, career orientation is clearly the *primary* basis for differences among military men. Career military men were, in terms of the substantive meanings of their mean scores, heavily promilitary concerning nearly all aspects of the military. Noncareer men were consistently different from their career counterparts (except for noncareer Army officers), and thus were much more mixed in their evaluation.

Third, rank also shows some important differences in attitudes among military men independent of their career orientation. Enlisted men, on the one hand, were somewhat more supportive of the use of military force. Officers, on the other hand, were somewhat more positive in their evaluation of the military organization. In terms of civil-military relations, officers were more likely to perceive military (versus civilian) influence to be low, but enlisted men were more likely to prefer greater military (versus civilian) influence. As a result, both saw military (versus civilian) influence to be inadequate, for somewhat different reasons. Noncareer men also saw military influence as inadequate, but to a lesser degree. In that respect, it is worth recalling that one of the most obvious differences between veterans and nonveterans was that veterans perceived military leaders to be rather low in influence.

Fourth, we have found that the hypothesized historical change in the cleavages within the military was supported by the 1972–73 Navy findings. Career orientation was a more important source of "ideological" cleavage than were rank differences. However, the findings for noncareer Army officers suggest that rank differences are once again coming to the fore with junior noncareer officers no longer being ideologically similar to junior noncareer enlisted men. If this is an indication of a secular trend—a shift from 1972–73 to 1974–75—then there may be at least two major kinds of consequences. The first consequence is that junior enlisted men who are not career oriented will be increasingly distinct as a group, with no authority figures that share their beliefs. Noncommissioned officers (the bulk of the career-oriented enlisted men), senior officers, and even most junior officers will all tend to differ from noncareer enlisted men in their views concerning the military and its mission. The second consequence is that there will be an increase in homogeneity of military men's belief systems as all the groups which wield either formal (officers) or informal (NCO's) organizational power come to show greater similarity in their beliefs. This question of homogeneity of beliefs will be examined in the next chapter.

Finally, we examined the issues of self-selection versus socialization. Although our findings cannot be definitive because of the cross-sectional nature of the samples, it appears that career/noncareer differences and the Army/Navy differences for noncareer officers are a reflection of the self-selecting process whereby men from primarily one part of the ideological spectrum choose to pursue careers in the military or to be officers in an all-volunteer situation.

5
Soldiers, Sailors, and Civilians: A Comparison

The Distinctiveness of the "Military Mind"

The distinctiveness of the military mind is generally accepted by critics (Mills, 1956; Perrucci and Pilisuk, 1971) as well as supporters (Huntington, 1957; Janowitz, 1960; Moskos, 1970) of the military. The argument, which is well developed in Abrahamsson (1972), is that the distinctiveness of the military mind comes as a result of it being a "professional mind" as compared to that of the general population. In addition, the military, in contrast to the general population, is thought to exhibit more *homogeneity* (as a result of the homogenization processes discussed in chapter 4) and a more *positive assessment* of its own profession. Janowitz (1960) also indicated that although higher education generally is linked to liberalism, the opposite is true for the professional military.

The specific distinctiveness of the military belief system is based on the nature of the military and its functions—the military way (Vagts, 1937). As professionals in violence (Janowitz, 1960), military men are part of an organizational system with the capacity to commit, and deal with the consequences of, large-scale, legitimate, collective violence (Van Doorn, 1976). The perspective of the military man is based on the willingness as well as the capacity to eliminate dysfunctional elements from the social (or organizational) system's environment (if so defined by legitimate authorities).

There are several problematic areas not adequately dealt with in most empirical analyses of the distinctiveness of military men's belief systems. Much of the past research on this question is too narrowly focused on military elites (Angell, 1965; Abrahamsson, 1968; Russett, 1974). Even when comparing civilian elites with the population as a whole the results show the distinctiveness of the elites (McClosky, 1958; Converse, 1964; Robinson and Hefner, 1968). Another problem has been the kinds of samples available (cf. Bengtsson, 1968). Consequently, the next step is to compare a broader sample of military men with their civilian peers.

The literature, then, argues persuasively for the distinctiveness of the belief system concerning the military found among military men. In the preceeding chapter we showed a distinction in belief systems between military men in our samples who were career oriented and those who were not. Hence, we expect that if this distinctiveness from civilians does in fact exist, it should show up primarily among career military men. In addition, we expect career officers, who have been most subject to the series of homogenization processes, to be the most distinguishable in terms of their beliefs about the military.

Civil-Military Comparisons: Selecting Matched Groups

In order to establish whether the beliefs found among military men really are distinctive, we need to compare military men with civilians. However, it is important to find *comparable* civilian groups. For example, Russett's (1974) study used two elite samples: the military elite consisted of military war college students from all the branches and was contrasted with a comparable level business elite.

In our study, we do not have elite military samples. Instead, we have representative cross sections of Army and

Navy men. Thus, we will attempt to find comparable groups from our civilian sample. In chapter 3 we saw that age and education were generally the most important civilian background characteristics in terms of predicting beliefs about the military. In chapter 4 we found that differences in such beliefs within the Army and Navy samples were most strongly linked to career orientation and rank.

For simplicity of data presentation and analysis, we compare several distinct groups of military personnel and civilians. The four military groups are familiar from the preceding chapter: career officers, noncareer officers, career enlisted men, and noncareer enlisted men. The civilian groups are defined in terms of their age and education but do not directly correspond to the civilian groups used in chapter 3.

Although the military groups are discrete in terms of their organizational characteristics (career orientation and rank), the groups overlap somewhat in terms of age and education. We have put together groups of civilians which match them in this respect in order to control for the effects of age and education in our comparisons. Noncareer enlisted men will be compared to all youth aged nineteen to twenty-four, noncareer officers to college graduates aged thirty-four or younger, career enlisted men to all non-college graduates (weighted for age) and career officers to all college graduates.[1]

---

1. Since only a small proportion of career men are over forty-five years of age, one could well question our leaving civilians over forty-five in the sample. Given that older civilians are, if anything, somewhat more promilitary, we felt that it made the crucial career men versus civilian comparisons even more conservative, i.e., more difficult to show differences, and was justifiable for comparisons of mean scores. However, the wider age gap could affect the standard deviations by artificially inflating those of the civilian groups used in comparisons later in the chapter. A separate examination of this issue showed that there were greater discrepancies in standard deviations by sex than by age, i.e., the overall standard deviation for a given group was more affected by whether both men and women were included than by whether more or less inclusive age groups were included. Thus, we proceeded in the fashion described in the text to maintain as many cases as possible, especially among the college graduates.

After comparing the age and education distributions for the matched military and civilian groups, we concluded that the civilian groups could be considered the age and education counterparts of the respective military groups. We use these groups both in our analysis of mean scores that follows and our later examination of standard deviations.

Civilian and Military Views of the Military

In chapter 4 we discussed the four military groups in terms of the relationships of their mean scores to the substantive midpoints of the sixteen measures. The focus of this analysis will be different. We will discuss the four groups in terms of the relationship of their mean scores to the mean scores of their civilian counterparts on the sixteen measures.

Enlisted Men and Their Civilian Counterparts

In the first two parts of figure 8 we have contrasted career and noncareer enlisted men with their civilian counterparts.[2] Several aspects of the data are particularly interesting. Part *A* of figure 8 shows that noncareer enlisted men did not hold consistently more favorable or unfavorable views of the military than did youth aged nineteen to twenty-four. They were more negative than civilians in their evaluation of the military organization. But they were more promilitary along some of the dimensions dealing with civil-military relations. This was especially true concerning military spending and perceptions of relative military versus civilian influence (which was also, then, reflected in evaluations of the adequacy of military influence). Equally interesting was the basic lack of difference concerning the use of military force, the views about citizen-soldiers, the range of viewpoints among servicemen, and amnesty.

---

2. Generally, a difference between career enlisted men (Army or Navy) and their civilian comparison group of more than .09 or .15 standard deviation is statistically significant at the p < .05 or p < .001 level (two-tailed) respectively. The comparable figures for noncareer EM/civilian differences are .15 and .25. See Bachman (1974, p. 27) for a discussion of significance testing with these samples.

Career enlisted men, on the other hand, were in most respects more promilitary than their civilian counterparts, as shown in part *B* of figure 8. This was especially true in terms of civil-military relations. Career men were more likely to want higher military spending and to perceive military influence as low (relative to civilian influence) and thus as inadequate. The conclusion to be drawn from these data is that career enlisted men were not only consistently different from noncareer enlisted men (as pointed out in chapter 4), but also consistently distinct from civilians of comparable age and education.

Officers and Their Civilian Counterparts

In parts *C* and *D* of figure 8 we have contrasted the mean scores of the noncareer and career officer groups with their respective civilian comparison groups.[3] The picture for career officers is very much like that for career enlisted men, but for noncareer officers the findings are more complex.

Career officers, as shown in part *D* of figure 8, were consistently more promilitary than their civilian comparison group, college graduates. This was true for nearly all aspects of the military. Officers viewed treatment in the services as being very fair and, not surprisingly, they viewed military leaders as quite competent. The officers, compared with civilian college graduates, also viewed civil-military relations in a very promilitary light, preferred higher military spending, and saw military (versus civilian) influence in military affairs as lower than it ought to be.

In views about the use of military force, career officers were generally much more interventionist than civilian college graduates, and also more supportive of the particular

---

3. Generally, a difference between career officers (Army or Navy) and their civilian comparison group of more than .19 or .32 standard deviation is statistically significant at the $p < .05$ or $p < .001$ level (two-tailed) respectively. The comparable figures for noncareer officer/civilian differences are .34 and .58 for the Army and .28 and .47 for the Navy (which reflects the small sizes of the officer and civilian samples for these groups).

intervention in Vietnam. However, they equalled or exceeded civilians in their opposition to obedience in a My Lai-type situation—an inappropriate and unprofessional use of military force.

The noncareer officers, as we noted in chapter 4, were the one category for which the Army data did not closely replicate the Navy data. Army noncareer officers were not all that sharply different from career officers in their mean scores (see figure 5). When we contrast Army noncareer officers with their civilian counterparts—younger college graduates—in part *C* of figure 8, their similarity to career officers is accentuated.

Navy noncareer officers, however, showed a more mixed set of ratings when compared to younger civilian college graduates. These officers saw military leaders as relatively low in influence (compared to civilian leaders), a perception held to an even stronger degree by the rest of the officer groups. Along some of the other dimensions the Navy noncareer officers were slightly more promilitary than their civilian counterparts, but along other dimensions the differences in means were very small or nonexistent. Certainly the overall impression is that this group of officers was not nearly so distinct from their civilian counterparts as were the other officer groups.

In summary, we find that career military men, both officers and enlisted men, were strongly and consistently more favorable to the military than were their civilian counterparts. Noncareer men showed fewer and less consistent differences; in some cases they were more promilitary than their civilian counterparts but in other cases they were not. Therefore, this mode of analysis provides considerable support for the military mind hypothesis, *but only for career men.*

Civilian Heterogeneity and Military Homogeneity in Beliefs

Our second approach in examining the differences of military beliefs from civilian beliefs is to look at the amount of

The Military Organization
   Perceived military job opportunities
   Perceived fair treatment in services
   Perceived competence of military leaders

Military Obedience
   Servicemen should obey without question
   Should obey in My Lai-type situation

Foreign Policy and Use of Force
   Support for military intervention
   Preference for U.S. military supremacy
   Support for U.S. actions in Vietnam

Civil-Military Relations
   Role of military seen as positive
   Preference for higher military spending
   Perceived military (vs. civilian) influence
   Preferred military (vs. civilian) influence
   Adequacy of military influence (perc.—pref.)
   Preference for citizen-soldiers
   Preferred wide range of views among servicemen
   Support for amnesty

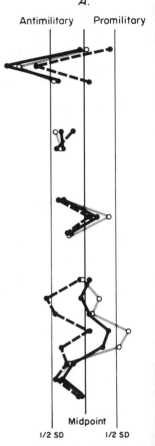

A.

Antimilitary   Promilitary

Midpoint
1/2 SD   1/2 SD

●—● Noncareer enlisted men—Nov
○—○ Noncareer enlisted men—Arm
●—● Civilian youth (age 19–24)

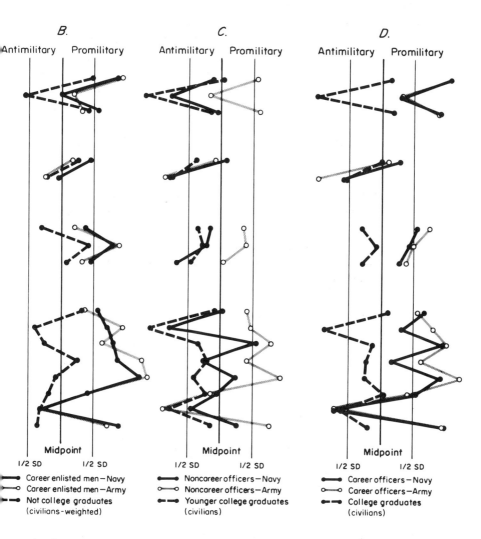

Fig. 8. Military groups contrasted with civilian counterparts. The data used to construct this figure are presented in tables 18, 19, and 20 in Appendix D.

variance in these beliefs as a measure of consensus or homogeneity. The homogenization processes presumed to be operating in the military should have effects not only on the location of mean scores but also on the size of the standard deviations (the square root of the variance). Standard deviations should be smaller among military men than among civilians. They should also be smaller among career men than among noncareer men. Finally, they should be smaller among officers than among enlisted men.

In tables 13 and 14 we have presented the standard deviations for the four Army groups, the four Navy groups, and six civilian groups. Although we did not find mean scores to be significantly different between men and women (see chapter 3), we did find some differences in standard deviations on the items. Women generally showed more homogeneity than did the men. Hence, where we have examined the standard deviations of *career* military groups (the groups most likely to be distinctive in this regard as they were for mean scores), we have presented the standard deviations for both men and women to control for sex differences. The nongraduates have not been weighted by age in this analysis, but have been combined to produce a single standard deviation for each sex group.

Noncareer Officers and Enlisted Men

In table 13 we can directly compare the standard deviations of noncareer men with those of their civilian age and educational peers. Differences between officers and younger college graduates in terms of which group has greater or lesser variance in their scores are mostly small and essentially random. Much the same holds true for noncareer enlisted men and youth aged nineteen to twenty-four. There seems little evidence that there were any consistent differences in the levels of homogeneity of civilians and those military men who were leaving the service.

Career Officers and Enlisted Men

The situation is quite different when we look at career military men and their civilian counterparts, male or female, in table 14. The pattern is very consistent among officers, and fairly consistent among enlisted men, to be more homogeneous than their civilian peers. Most of the exceptions to that rule involve the women's standard deviations. In addition, we can see very consistent differences between officers and enlisted men, a pattern not found among comparable civilian groups (the differences between college graduates and nongraduates seem to be essentially random).

There is one more comparison to make using tables 13 and 14. That comparison is between career men and noncareer men. For both officers and enlisted men, there were fairly consistent differences between those who were career oriented and those who were not. Career-oriented men showed more consensus or homogeneity in their beliefs than did noncareer men.

Summary and Conclusions

In this chapter we have examined the basic question of whether military men are distinctive from civilians in their beliefs concerning the military. To do so, we have applied two different types of data analysis in which we directly contrasted Army and Navy subgroups with their civilian counterparts (matched for age and education).

First, we contrasted the mean scores of four Army and four Navy groups, defined by career orientation and rank, with the mean scores of civilian groups comparable in age and education. We found that *career* men, both officers and enlisted, were consistently more promilitary than their civilian age and education counterparts. Noncareer men were in some respects more promilitary than their civilian counterparts, but in other respects they were not. In particular, noncareer men were more promilitary on issues of civil-military relations, e.g., military spending, perceptions of

TABLE 13

Standard Deviations for Noncareer-Oriented Military Men and Civilian Comparison Groups

	Noncareer Officers		Younger College Graduates (N=116)	Noncareer Enlisted Men		Youth Aged 19-24 (N=249)
	Navy (N=85)	Army (N=45)		Navy (N=1134)	Army (N=887)	
The Military Organization						
Perceived military job opportunities	.75	.92	.85	.82	.98	.88
Perceived fair treatment in services	.92	.92	.85	.82	.92	.91
Perceived competence of military leaders	.91	.81	.94	.90	.97	1.03
Military Obedience						
Servicemen should obey without question	.85	.97	.84	.93	.98	.97
Should obey in My Lai-type situation	.68	.68	.72	.74	.80	.76
Foreign Policy and Use of Force						
Support for military intervention	.75	.72	.66	.79	.83	.75
Preference for U.S. military supremacy	.86	.80	.75	.87	.87	.88
Support for U.S. actions in Vietnam	.69	.74	.67	.65	.63	.70
Civil-Military Relations						
Role of military seen as positive	.75	.67	.73	.71	.79	.77
Preference for higher military spending	.93	.84	.85	1.18	1.22	.98
Perceived military (vs. civilian) influence	.82	.74	1.04	1.04	1.01	1.02
Preferred military (vs. civilian) influence	.65	.64	.72	.78	.86	.82
Adequacy of military influence (perc. – pref.)	1.20	.95	1.27	1.38	1.38	1.44
Preference for citizen-soldiers	.90	.75	.79	.85	.80	.78
Preferred wide range of views among servicemen	.70	.80	.71	.76	.72	.75
Support for amnesty	1.04	.83	1.12	1.08	1.13	1.08

TABLE 14

Standard Deviations for Career-Oriented Military Men and Civilian Comparison Groups

	Career Officers		College Graduates		Career Enlisted Men		Nongraduates	
	Navy (N=223)	Army (N=194)	Men (N=133)	Women (N=109)	Navy (N=867)	Army (N=934)	Men (N=583)	Women (N=887)
The Military Organization								
Perceived military job opportunities	.69	.63	.91	.76	.79	.82	.88	.88
Perceived fair treatment in services	.85	.85	.91	.73	.87	.98	.92	.82
Perceived competence of military leaders	.75	.65	.99	.91	.86	.89	1.01	.82
Military Obedience								
Servicemen should obey without question	.68	.83	.96	.90	.80	.95	.96	.96
Should obey in My Lai-type situation	.75	.61	.84	.59	.76	.84	.80	.68
Foreign Policy and Use of Force								
Support for military intervention	.71	.72	.75	.80	.81	.91	.80	.79
Preference for U.S. military supremacy	.74	.73	.83	.89	.70	.74	.89	.84
Support for U.S. actions in Vietnam	.63	.63	.75	.82	.63	.68	.72	.70
Civil-Military Relations								
Role of military seen as positive	.54	.64	.73	.68	.62	.72	.73	.61
Preference for higher military spending	.84	.73	.85	.85	.89	.90	.95	.84
Perceived military (vs. civilian) influence	.72	.52	1.04	1.12	.87	.96	1.01	1.08
Preferred military (vs. civilian) influence	.59	.66	.83	.68	.72	.73	.87	.80
Adequacy of military influence (perc.–pref.)	.92	.88	1.30	1.36	1.09	1.19	1.32	1.27
Preference for citizen-soldiers	.77	.72	.88	.83	.82	.77	.83	.84
Preferred wide range of views among servicemen	.72	.78	.86	.73	.78	.79	.80	.80
Support for amnesty	.70	.62	1.15	1.08	.80	.89	1.06	1.08

military versus civilian influence (and, thus, adequacy of military influence). They were generally quite similar to their civilian counterparts on most other issues, except that noncareer enlisted men were more negative about the military organization than their civilian peers. All in all, we conclude that this evidence for military distinctiveness in beliefs is convincing, but only for career men.

Second, we examined measures of dispersion among responses in order to assess the level of consensus or homogeneity among military men and civilians on the various issues measured. Once again, career men showed a distinctiveness that was not found among noncareer men. Career men displayed more homogeneity than their civilian counterparts, with career *officers* showing the highest level of homogeneity. We found no evidence (in Blair, 1975) that this greater homogeneity among career men is a function of age, and no substantial evidence that the differences between officers and enlisted men are a function of education.[4]

We conclude that there is considerable evidence that the belief system of career military men, officers and enlisted, is distinctive from that found among comparable civilian groups. Career men were considerably more promilitary and also showed greater homogeneity or consensus in these beliefs. The same is not true for noncareer men, who did not show any consistent pattern of distinctiveness from their civilian counterparts. This finding is wholly consistent with the views of Janowitz (1960) and of Huntington (1957).

One of the arguments raised in the debate about the all-volunteer force was the danger of a "separate military

---

4. A third and more subtle kind of evidence for distinctiveness in the belief systems of military men would have been to find that the factor structures were different for military groups as contrasted to civilian groups. As the data included in Appendix B indicate, we did not find such differences. If we had, there would have been some question as to whether our questionnaire items had the same patterns of meaning for military men as for civilians. Thus, we were not altogether disappointed by the lack of differences along this dimension, especially given the fairly clear and straightforward findings from our comparison of means and standard deviations.

ethos" or a distinctive "military mind" brought about by a military force made up largely of career men. The findings presented above suggest some basis for concern in this area. To the extent that new recruits into an all-volunteer force consist more and more of the type of career-oriented personnel we have been studying here, it seems inevitable that the military will become more separated from civilians, at least when it comes to views about the military and its mission.

In thinking about this problem of ideological representativeness, one can pose two "ideal or pure types" of military forces—the citizen force and the career force. These types can be thought of as the two ends of a continuum. In other words, the opposite of a career force made up primarily of career-oriented personnel would be a citizen force made up very largely of citizen-soldiers (or sailors, etc.) who view their tour of military duty as a temporary activity, a part of their citizenship.

Neither type of force has existed in pure form in the United States. There has always been a career component of "professionals" and "lifers" as well as a citizen component of "in-and-outers." In particular, it would not be accurate to describe the U.S. military of the recent past as a citizen force. Rather, it was what the president's commission termed a mixed force, consisting of some conscripts, some draft-motivated enlistees, and some so-called true volunteers.

But what kind of force are we going to have with no conscription to guarantee a large citizen component? In other words, where will the all-volunteer force lie on the continuum? To the extent that an all-volunteer force comes to consist largely or primarily of career-oriented men (and women), and thus approximates in reality our career force, the attitudes found among its members as a whole will be increasingly discrepant from those found among civilians. If this is the future of the all-volunteer force, it will be considerably less ideologically representative than was the mixed force of the past.

6

Views about Military versus Civilian Influence

What role do military leaders play in the making of national-security policy? In which policy areas are they more influential than civilian leaders? In which areas is their influence less? And apart from the way things may actually be, who *should* have more influence in major decisions involving the military and national security, civilian leaders or military leaders?

These are the types of questions to be treated in this chapter. Our purpose is not to attempt objective answers. Instead, we will continue to examine the survey data obtained from military men and civilians and focus on their *perceptions* of what the policy-making role of military leaders is, and also their *preferences* about what that role should be. Conflicting hypotheses concerning the consequences of military professionalization also will be examined: Huntington's (1957) hypothesis of professional neutrality and acceptance of civilian control versus Abrahamsson's (1972) hypothesis of a quest for professional autonomy and political role expansion.

There has been much scholarly debate about the extent to which military leaders are influential in policy making. Mills (1956) saw the military as the most powerful participant in the military industrial complex. Although equally critical of the role of the military industrial complex in foreign policy making, Domhoff (1967) and Kolko (1969) saw the military as a relatively noninfluential member. Indeed, Janowitz (1971) and Segal and Segal (1971) described military leaders as "junior partners" in the military industrial complex, and in policy making generally, and have indicated that military men see themselves as relatively powerless. Abrahamsson (1972) and Larson (1974) have commented on the military's low level of professional autonomy.

Military Professionalization and Its Consequences

There has been considerable disagreement concerning the consequences of professionalization for the military's political neutrality and willingness to submit to civilian control. Huntington (1957) argued that professionalization would lead to professional detachment from politics and contribute to civilian control over the military through the internalization of "professional" values by military men.

Janowitz (1971) argued that such internal control mechanisms are inadequate and must be supplemented by powerful external constraints imposed by the executive, congressional, and judiciary branches of government. Abrahamsson (1972) argued that the process of professionalization leads inevitably to the development of a corporate interest group which will seek to increase its professional autonomy and expand its political role. Specifically, he hypothesized that the internalization of norms restricting the military's political role, as hypothesized by Huntington, would be exactly the opposite of what one should expect the process of professionalization to produce.

Military professionalization is relevant to two somewhat different aspects of the military's political role. The first aspect of that role deals with the different areas or domains of national-security policy. These can be thought of as arrayed on a continuum from distinctly military to distinctly civilian. For example, specific battlefield tactics may be thought of as primarily a military policy area, whereas the decision of whether to become involved in an international conflict in the first place may be regarded as essentially a civilian policy domain.

Both the historical process of professionalization and the individual professional development of military men should lead to careful distinctions between military and civilian policy domains according to Huntington's hypotheses. More professionalized military men (career officers in particular) should be more able and willing than are civilians or noncareer military men to differentiate between that which is essentially military and that which is primarily civilian.

The second aspect of the military's political role involves the evaluation of the adequacy of military participation in *each* policy domain. Such evaluations are based on the perception of current levels of influence as well as on preferences for what levels should exist. To accept Huntington's image of the willing military servant of civilian political leaders would be to argue that even if military men perceived the political influence of their leaders to be low in a given area of policy, they would accept that as appropriate and hence not view military influence as inadequate. Accepting Abrahamsson's view of the military as a corporate interest group seeking professional autonomy and political role expansion would lead one to quite different predictions. One would predict that perceptions of low relative influence of military leaders vis-à-vis civilian leaders would be coupled with the desire of more influence and, hence, military influence would be evaluated as inadequate among military men.

In this chapter we argue, consistent with Abrahamsson's hypothesis, that military men perceive military versus civilian influence to be low in nearly all areas of national-security policy, noting at the same time that they prefer it to be considerably greater. Hence, they evaluate the role of military leaders as *inadequate.* We consider the findings that we present to be indicators of a desire by military men for an *expansion of their political role* in all areas of national security policy, i.e., a reflection of their desire to be more than "junior partners."

Civilian Perceptions and Preferences

Among the variables treated in the preceding chapters are three composite measures dealing with military versus civilian influence—perceived military influence, preferred military influence, and adequacy of military influence (the gap between perception and preference). In the present chapter we dissect these composite measures of civil-military influence and examine the specific items on which they are based. Respondents were asked to rate amounts of military versus civilian influence in each of five areas: U.S. involvement in foreign conflicts, battlefield tactics, choice of new weapon systems, military pay levels, and use of nuclear weapons. For each area, respondents gave two ratings: a *perception* of present conditions ("this is how I think it is now"), and a *preference* ("this is how I'd like it to be").

Civilian responses to these questionnaire items are summarized in figure 9. On the average, the civilians showed a great deal of satisfaction with the status quo as they perceived it. Their mean ratings of perceived and preferred influence were virtually identical. They rated military leaders as having somewhat more influence over tactics than civilians, and considered that level of influence the way things ought to be. They also tended to see military leaders as a bit more influential than civilians in deciding which new weapon systems to develop, and they preferred it that way. In such other matters as military pay, foreign involvements, and the use of nuclear weapons, the average civilian respondent rated military and civilian leaders as about equal in influence; and apparently this is also what the average respondent preferred.

The tendency for civilians to be satisfied with the status quo is consistent with the finding that over one-half the people in a recent national sample said the level of military influence in society should be "the same as now," with the rest of the sample split just about evenly between those who preferred more military influence and those who preferred less. Nevertheless, it is startling to find that civilians in

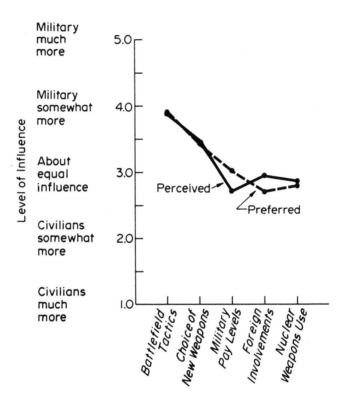

Fig. 9. Civilian views on military versus civilian influence. The data used to construct this figure are presented in table 21 in Appendix D.

1972–73 were so willing to see military and civilian leaders as having equal influence over the involvement of troops in foreign conflicts or the use of nuclear weapons, since by law these are clearly areas of civilian control.

Of course, the civilian satisfaction with the status quo applies only on the average. Some respondents perceived military influence to be higher than the level they would prefer, and a roughly equal number took the opposite view. We noted in chapter 3 that views about military versus civilian influence were related to the respondents' past military experience; veterans perceived actual levels of military influence to be somewhat lower than did nonveterans. Other differences in viewpoints were related to age and education. Younger respondents *perceived* higher levels of military influence than did older ones, on the average. And those with higher levels of education were more likely to *prefer* rather low levels of military influence.

The age and education differences noted above appear somewhat consistently across all five areas of influence treated in the questionnaire. Figure 10 presents the data for the two "extreme" age and education subgroups—younger (age 34 or less) college graduates and older nongraduates. (The results of the other two age/education subgroups lie between these two groups; mean scores for all four groups are presented in Appendix D.) When we look at the scores for the younger college graduates, we see that on every dimension except military pay, the preferred level of military influence was lower than the level actually perceived to exist. Among older nongraduates just the opposite pattern appeared although the discrepancies were not as large.

Another observation based on the data shown in figure 10 is perhaps more subtle, but worth noting. The younger college graduates were relatively discriminating in their ratings of the five different areas of influence, i.e., there was a fairly substantial gap between their preferences about battlefield tactics and their preferences about foreign involvements and nuclear weapons. The older graduates had less differentiated preferences. The noncollege graduates, both

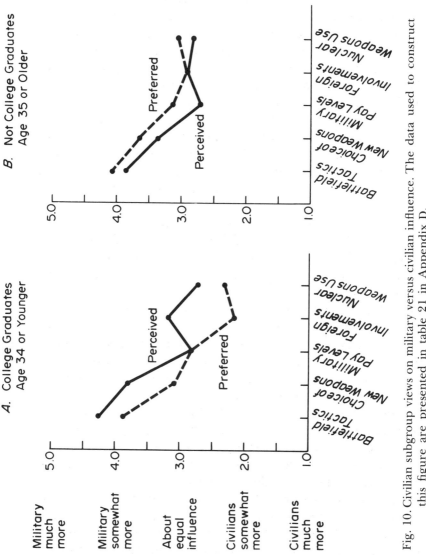

Fig. 10. Civilian subgroup views on military versus civilian influence. The data used to construct this figure are presented in table 21 in Appendix D.

younger and older, apparently were less discriminating in their preferences for the different influence areas.

Perceptions and Preferences of Military Men

We turn now to the perceptions and preferences of military men along the same dimensions we have been discussing for civilians. We will continue to distinguish among four categories of military men:

noncareer-oriented enlisted men
career-oriented enlisted men
noncareer-oriented officers
career-oriented officers

And we will present data from both the 1972–73 Navy sample and the 1974–75 Army sample. The mean questionnaire responses for these groups of military men are displayed in the four parts of figure 11. An examination of this figure leads to a number of comments and conclusions.

1. The perceived and preferred influence ratings are in much the same order for each set of military respondents. Moreover, the ordering is similar to that found for civilians in figure 9. (The sequence in which the items are presented in all of the figures reflects this ordering; it is not the sequence in which the questions were asked.) All military and civilian subgroups rated battlefield tactics as the area of greatest military influence (among those listed), while the areas of greatest civilian influence were seen to be decisions about foreign involvements and the use of nuclear weapons.

   The area of pay levels and fringe benefits in the armed services deserves special mention. Among all four categories of career and noncareer officers and enlisted men, this was the area of the greatest dissatisfaction with the status quo, i.e., the greatest dis-

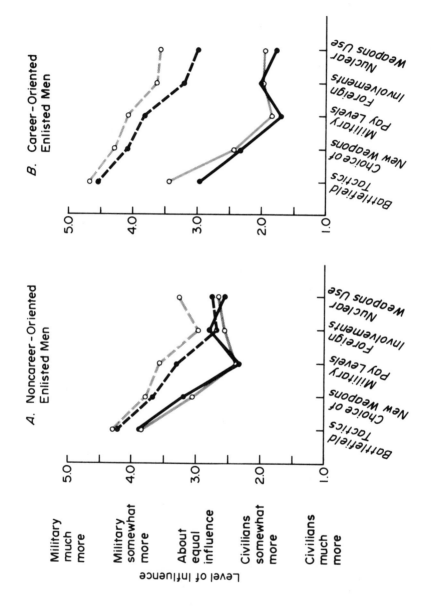

A. Noncareer-Oriented Enlisted Men

B. Career-Oriented Enlisted Men

Level of Influence

Military much more
Military somewhat more
About equal influence
Civilians somewhat more
Civilians much more

Battlefield Tactics
Choice of New weapons
Military Pay Levels
Foreign Involvements
Nuclear Weapons Use

5.0
4.0
3.0
2.0
1.0

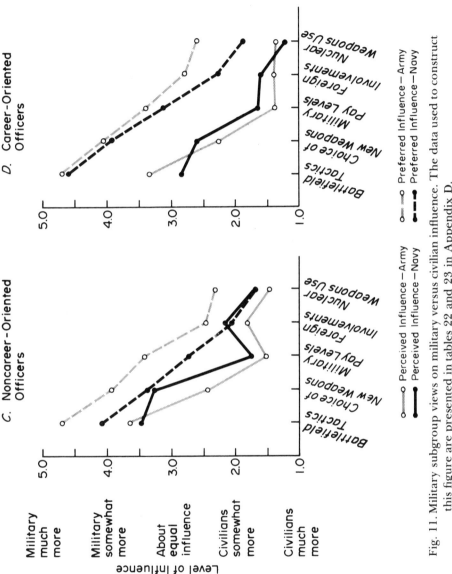

Fig. 11. Military subgroup views on military versus civilian influence. The data used to construct this figure are presented in tables 22 and 23 in Appendix D.

crepancy between ratings of the way things are and the way they ought to be. Military men, on the one hand, perceived this as an area of somewhat greater civilian influence, whereas they preferred that the greater amount of influence be exercised by military leaders. Civilians, on the other hand, both perceived and preferred about equal civilian and military influence over military pay and fringe benefits.

2. Military officers, both career and noncareer, tended to make much sharper discriminations among the various areas of influence than did the enlisted men. This tendency showed up to some extent in their ratings of the way things actually are, but was especially strong in their statements about the way they preferred things to be. On the one hand, they thought there should be a good deal more military than civilian influence over choice of battlefield tactics. However, their responses here were not sharply different from the preferences expressed by enlisted men, or for that matter, by civilians. On the other hand, when it came to foreign involvements and the use of nuclear weapons, the officers, like the civilian college graduates, preferred more emphasis on civilian decision making. (There are some distinctions to be made between Army and Navy officers, and those who did and did not have military career plans; we will turn to such distinctions below.)

No doubt officers have had occasion to give these matters much more thought and study than either enlisted men or the average civilian. The result is that officers were more discriminating in their ratings and far more willing to grant decision-making priorities to civilians in the areas that are traditionally civilian. Lest we conclude, however, that military officers are unique in this respect, we should recall that civilian college graduates were equal to officers in their preferences for greater civilian than military control over foreign involvements and nuclear weapons. Indeed, if we concentrate on *discrepancies* between ratings of "how I think it is now" and "how I'd like it to be," we see that civilian college graduates preferred a reduction in military influence in these areas whereas most officers preferred an increase.

3. If we view discrepancies between the perception and preference ratings as a reflection of dissatisfaction with the status quo, the career enlisted men were by far the most dissatisfied group of respondents we have examined. They preferred a good deal of military influence over all areas, even (in the case of the Army career enlisted men) extending to predominantly military influence over foreign involvements and decisions about the use of nuclear weapons.

Career officers, while more discriminating in their influence ratings, were a close second to career enlisted men in their discrepancies between perceptions of "how it is now" and their preferences for how they would "like it to be." Both categories of career men are especially noteworthy in terms of their perceptions of actual levels of military versus civilian influence. Career military men, both officers and enlisted men, Army and Navy, tended to see military leaders as much less influential than civilian leaders. This is somewhat different from the perceptions of noncareer military men, and it stands in sharp contrast to the perceptions of the civilian respondents.

One way of viewing the discrepancies between perceptions and preferences is to say that career men in the military tend to feel relatively powerless as a group over decisions that vitally affect their lives. They see decisions as being made mostly by civilians rather than by their own leaders. But why is it that career-oriented servicemen rated actual levels of military influence so much lower than did noncareer enlisted men and especially civilians? Is it because the relatively inexperienced noncareer enlisted men and also the civilian respondents are simply unrealistic about the actual levels of military versus civilian influence? Or does it mean that the career men are overly frustrated about what they perceive to be inadequate levels of military influence? To put the matter another way, should we conceive of the ratings of actual influence as more-or-less dispassionate reports of the way things are, or should we view them primarily as attitudinal measures—indicators of dissatisfaction and a sense of relative powerlessness among some military men? These questions are not purely speculative; earlier analyses of some of these data (Bachman, 1973, 1974) have indicated that the measures of perceived military influence "act like" other more clearly attitudinal dimensions, i.e., they appear to be a part of the overall pattern of pro- or antimilitary sentiment discussed in earlier chapters. Thus we conclude that the military men's ratings of actual influence levels are, at least in part, an indirect indication of dissatisfaction with the status quo.

In sum, it seems that career officers and enlisted men thought there should be a substantial increase in military influence across the range of decision making, from battlefield tactics to the use of military weapons. Some critics have argued that an all-volunteer military force will involve a heavier reliance on career men, thereby encouraging a "separate military ethos" which would constitute a political threat. This desire on the part of career men for increased military influence over national decision making can hardly be reassuring to such critics.

4. We turn now to a comparison of influence ratings by Navy men in 1972–73 and those by Army men in 1974–75. Here, as we noted for the broader range of measures discussed in chapter 4, the similarities between the two samples far outweigh the differ-

ences. For three of the four subgroups, the Army responses very closely replicate the ones obtained two years earlier from the Navy sample. The largest discrepancies appeared again between Army and Navy noncareer officers, and these differences were larger for preferences about influence than for perceptions of actual influence levels. Army noncareer officers preferred somewhat higher levels of military influence than did their Navy counterparts.

The other three subgroups also showed some tendency for Army men to prefer slightly higher levels of military influence than did Navy men. These differences showed up in the area of foreign involvements and especially in decisions about the use of nuclear weapons. Whether this reflects some difference between the two service branches or whether this reflects a more general shift in the thinking of military men during the two-year interval between the Navy and Army data collections cannot be known from these data alone.

Summary and Conclusions

In this chapter we have taken a detailed look at a series of questions dealing with the influence of military leaders and civilian leaders. The questions deal with matters ranging from such broad strategic issues as U.S. involvement in foreign conflict and the use of nuclear weapons, on the one hand, to more specific issues such as battlefield tactics. In each case respondents were asked for their perceptions about actual distribution of influence between military and civilian leaders, and also for their preferences about the distribution of influence. These two kinds of questions make it possible to consider still another kind of dimension—the gap or discrepancy between perception and preference, which can be treated as a measure of the adequacy of military influence.

Civilian responses to these questions, taken as a whole, suggest that in 1973 there was a good deal of satisfaction with the status quo. In other words, the average levels of military influence preferred by civilians came very close to the average perceptions about the amounts of influence actually existing. They perceived that military leaders were just about equal to civilian leaders in making decisions about foreign conflicts and the use of nuclear weapons; and in other areas, military leaders were perceived to be more influential than civilian leaders. Perhaps the fact that many civilians seemed to like things that way should be interpreted as a vote of confidence in military leaders, or a vote of no confidence in civilian leaders (in the aftermath of the Vietnam War), or some combination of both. Whatever the explanation, these data suggest a willingness on the part of the general public to give military leaders an equal share in areas of decision making which are traditionally and constitutionally the responsibility of civilian leaders.

Of course, when civilian respondents are separated according to age and education, some differences in viewpoint emerge. Those with higher levels of education preferred somewhat less in the way of military influence, and the younger respondents were more apt to see the actual levels of military influence as rather high. Thus it follows that the younger college-educated respondents preferred less military influence than they perceived to be the current situation, whereas the opposite was true for older respondents who were not college educated.

Noncareer enlisted men in both Army and Navy samples showed a pattern of perceptions and preferences similar to the pattern for the total civilian sample. Some gap appeared between perceptions and preferences, with the noncareer servicemen preferring a bit more military influence than they perceived to be the case. Nevertheless, the discrepancy was not very large. The noncareer officers in the 1972–73 Navy sample also showed a tendency to prefer moderately more military influence than they thought presently existed. However, among the Army noncareer officers surveyed in 1974–75 the gap between perception and preference was appreciably larger.

But the largest and most consistent discrepancies between perceptions and preferences about military influence were found among those officers and enlisted men who had career interests in the military. Although the career-oriented officers were more discriminating in their ratings of the different areas than were the career-oriented enlisted men, both groups perceived actual levels of military influence as being quite low and preferred that they be much higher.

How do these findings relate to the theoretical issues we considered at the start of this chapter? For one thing, it seems clear that professional military men perceived military leaders to be very junior partners in policy making. This perception coincides with the way Huntington (1957) thinks things should be. But the career military men themselves preferred quite another state of affairs. These preferences match Abrahamsson's (1972) view that increased professionalization will lead military personnel to desire a greater role in policy making. To the extent that such preferences for greater military influence become reflected in political activity, the assumption of political neutrality in Huntington's model of objective civilian control of the military fails to be fulfilled.

At a less theoretical level, it seems worth noting that the responses of career-oriented military men reported here are in several respects quite unusual for survey data. A number of their mean scores are extremely close to one end or other of the five-point response scale—something which has no parallel in the data for civilians or noncareer military men. Moreover, the mean discrepancies between their perceptions and their preferences are almost all strikingly large. In short, the career military men were telling us— louder and clearer than we are accustomed to hearing—that they were dissatisfied with present levels of military influence and preferred a good deal more. These findings raise anew our concerns about civilian control of the military— especially under all-volunteer conditions which seem to be encouraging a higher proportion of career-oriented men and women in the armed forces.

7
Summary, Conclusions, and Policy Implications

We stated at the outset that this volume is concerned with two interrelated questions: Who should serve in the all-volunteer military force in the United States? and What should be the relationship between the military and the civilian society? In the early chapters we provided a theoretical and historical context within which to examine these issues. Then we reported in considerable detail the results of three major surveys: a cross section of civilians in early 1973; a sample of Navy personnel in 1972–73; and a sample of Army personnel in 1974–75. In this chapter we summarize our findings and conclusions derived from the survey data, then we spell out what we consider to be the most important policy implications based on these findings.

Summary of Findings and Conclusions

In all three surveys we found that attitudes about the military and its mission were intercorrelated. In other words, those individuals who were most favorable toward the military along one dimension tended to be among the more favorable, or less critical, along other dimensions. For example, those who rated military leadership as highly competent also expressed lower than average criticism of military budgets. Given this fairly strong pattern of intercorrelations among different ratings of the military and its mission, we have found it useful to speak in terms of a general factor of promilitary (or antimilitary) sentiment, and have referred to some groups as being more promilitary than other groups. Now let us consider the findings for some of these different groups.

Civilian Views of the Military

Chapter 3 summarizes civilian views about the military, as reflected in the questionnaire data collected from the national sample of civilians early in 1973. In that chapter several different themes are stressed.

One theme is that public ratings of the military in 1973 reflected a mixture of positive and negative feelings, depending upon the dimension being considered. The evaluation of the *military organization* was generally favorable. Yet, there was considerable reluctance to support the *use of military force* except in self-defense. In the area of *civil-military relations,* we found mostly positive ratings of the military role in society and the level of military versus civilian influence. Nevertheless, a majority of respondents were critical of waste, inefficiency, and excess spending in the military.

Evaluations of the military and its mission varied somewhat across different groups. Younger college graduates as a group not only called the use of military force into question, but also were critical of virtually all aspects of the military organization and existing civil-military relations as well. However, older noncollege graduates as a group showed predominantly promilitary attitudes, but were still critical of the use of military force for intervention, high levels of military spending, and the fairness of treatment within the military. There was strong majority support for the concept of the all-volunteer force and relatively little concern about some of the issues which have been raised as potential problems. The nationwide civilian sample supported the all-volunteer approach rather than the draft by nearly a two-to-one margin. There was also very strong support for higher military pay levels considered to be necessary under a volunteer system.

When asked about issues related to the types of people who would staff the military services, there was a slight tendency for people to favor citizen-soldiers over career men, but the views seemed rather mixed. Civilian responses to open-ended interview items about the all-volunteer force left a dominant impression that the general public has not thought much about the question of what kinds of people will, or should, staff an all-volunteer armed force.

Military Men View the Military

Our examination of belief systems concerning the military found among military men has been based on the sample of Navy personnel surveyed in late 1972 and early 1973, and the sample of Army personnel surveyed in late 1974 and early 1975. The findings are detailed in chapters 4 and 5. A few of the highlights are noted here.

First of all, we failed to find a clear and uniform promilitary stance *among the military men as a whole*. There were substantial differences among our military respondents—they were not all of a single "military mind."

Second, it appears that the most important factor in accounting for variations in military views is career orientation. Those who had career interests in the military were, on the average, enthusiastically promilitary along virtually every dimension. Noncareer men, however, were quite different from their career counterparts in most respects; their ratings of the military were much more mixed.

Third, we found that the Army data collected in 1974–75 replicated the 1972–73 Navy data in most respects. The findings for enlisted men were highly similar. In both branches the career-oriented enlisted men were strongly promilitary, whereas the noncareer enlisted men were not. (In fact, the noncareer enlisted men were quite critical of the military in terms of leadership competence and fair treatment.) Among the officers, career-oriented men in both the Army and the Navy were quite promilitary, while noncareer officers in the Navy were distinctly less favorable. The noncareer Army officers, however, were almost as promilitary as career officers, thus failing to replicate the Navy findings.

Soldiers, Sailors and Civilians: A Comparison

Chapter 5 compares career and noncareer officers and enlisted men with civilians, more specifically, with subgroups of the civilian sample that match each military group fairly closely in terms of age and education. Since military groups differ in age and education, and since both of these dimensions were related to civilian views about the military, the matched group analyses were seen as a way to separate uniquely military aspects of ideology from those having to do with age and education. The results are fully consistent with the findings summarized above.

The noncareer military men were in many respects not very different from their civilian counterparts. Noncareer enlisted men were quite similar to civilians aged nineteen through twenty-four in their views about foreign policy, military power, Vietnam, amnesty, citizen-soldiers, and their overall rating of the military in society. In other areas, however, there were some differences. The noncareer enlisted men were more critical than their civilian counterparts in ratings of military working conditions and the competence of officers; but they were more promilitary than the young civilians in their preferences for military spending and higher military (versus civilian) influence over decisions involving national military policy. Noncareer Navy officers were also similar to their civilian counterparts (in this case college graduates aged 34 or younger); however, noncareer officers in the Army were consistently more promilitary than the civilians.

Military men with career interests were much more promilitary than their civilian counterparts. The findings are especially strong in the case of career officers. Because the great majority of officers are college graduates, we contrasted them with civilian college graduates. Since, within the civilian sample, college graduates are generally *less* favorable to the military, the contrast with career officers is particularly striking. Compared with their educational peers in civilian life, the career officers are a great deal more favorable toward the military organization, more eager for U.S. military supremacy (rather than parity with the Soviet Union), more willing to make use of military power, and much more in favor of enlarged military (versus civilian) influence over U.S. policy affecting the military.

At several points in our analysis we referred to the issue of military versus civilian influence. Civilian response to this issue showed, in the aggregate, a good deal of satisfaction with what they perceived to be the balance of military versus civilian influence. It is not surprising to find that civilians rate military leaders as more influential than civilians in determining battlefield tactics, nor is it surprising that they preferred things that way. What *is* surprising is that the average civilian respondent rated military and civilian leaders as being about equally influential in such traditionally (and legally) "civilian control" areas as involving U.S. servicemen in foreign conflicts or deciding whether to use nuclear weapons. Still more interesting is the finding that the civilian respondents liked it that way.

If civilians, on the average, were satisfied with the status quo as they perceived it, military men surely were not. This is one area in which both career and noncareer Army and Navy men preferred to see change. Having said that, we must immediately add that there were substantial and rather interesting differences between career and noncareer men and between officers and enlisted men in their responses to these questions. Nevertheless, all of the military groups preferred at least somewhat more military (versus civilian) influence than they perceived presently existed.

The career military men, in particular, to a far greater degree than noncareer men, preferred an across-the-board increase in military influence. Both career officers and career enlisted men rated military leaders as being less influential than civilians in all areas except battlefield tactics (where they were rated equal); and both groups thought the level of military influence should be substantially increased. The findings are much stronger than are usually found on survey scales of this sort (and much stronger than the findings for civilians or noncareer military men). If the findings are to be taken at all seriously, they indicate a profound sense of dissatisfaction among career military men, i.e., they feel that their own kind, the top military leaders, should have more power over national-military policy than civilian leaders.

Why Career Military Men Are Different:
Attitude Change or Self-selection?

We have noted that career military men are, on the average, ideologically different from their civilian counterparts and also from noncareer military men. It is important to consider why this pattern of differences in attitudes occurs. We have distinguished two possible explanations, each of which may be true to some degree.

1. During the early years of military experience, those individuals who will later reenlist undergo *attitude change* in a more promilitary direction—a process of "socialization into the military."
2. Prior to enlistment, some individuals are more promilitary than others, and these differences are influential in the *self-selection* process reflected in the decision to reenlist.

Our data did not permit a thorough test of these two alternative explanations. However, we are able to shed some light on the matter. Our analysis suggests that the dominant role is played by self-selection, that is, individuals on the promilitary side of the ideological spectrum are the ones most likely to pursue careers in the military. If we may anticipate our discussion of policy implications, it would seem that if we are concerned about maintaining some degree of ideological balance in the all-volunteer force, we may need to take *special* pains to ensure that military recruits represent a broad ideological cross section. In the following pages we suggest some ways in which this might be done.

Policy Issues and Implications

The research summarized here, based on a comparison of Army, Navy, and civilian samples, has shown important ideological differences between career military men and their noncareer or civilian counterparts. We think these differences may have implications for the all-volunteer force.

Under present conditions, an all-volunteer force in general, and the ground combat forces in particular, are likely to recruit and retain personnel from only part of the ideological range found in the civilian population. The very individuals who are needed to broaden the ideological balance are probably the least likely to enlist or to reenlist. If the nation's leaders value the concept of the citizen-soldier or sailor, they would do well to broaden the incentives in ways that are especially attractive to those presently underrepresented among volunteers. And, in spite of the additional costs involved, it would be wise to seek out more enlistees who are likely to serve for one term only and then return to civilian life.

What Kinds of Recruits and How to Recruit Them?

Career military men, and those most likely to become career men, tend to be somewhat more zealous about the military than their civilian age mates. This is one of the strongest and most consistent findings in our research. There is much to indicate that these differences are due, at least in part, to processes of self-selection.

How should military recruiting efforts respond to the finding that enlistees and especially career men are likely to come from only a limited ideological range? One approach is to embrace this state of affairs enthusiastically, assuming that the more promilitary individuals are likely to be less troublesome and more in agreement with traditional military values and practices than some of their less gung ho contemporaries. Indeed, the idea of concentrating recruitment efforts on those most favorably disposed toward the military is one of the specific recommendations in a recent report that introduced the concept of the "quality man" to the Army. Quality man is defined as an individual who, among other things, says that he places high importance on patriotism, is proud of being an American, would be among the first to defend the country if it were attacked, and is generally more favorable toward military service (Opinion Research Corporation, 1974).

The approach of aiming recruitment efforts toward the more gung ho is understandably tempting to recruiters and perhaps to many others in the military. And it may appear to be successful in the short run. But in our view, such a recruiting approach would be unwise in the long run. It would tend to reinforce and heighten the tendencies we have already observed for career military men to be less than fully representative of the cross section of civilian viewpoints. By strengthening support for some unnecessary and perhaps counterproductive military traditions and practices, or at least reducing resistance to them, this approach could gradually widen the gap between the military and the civilian world. We suspect that this gap would eventually reduce the supply of recruits below an acceptable level. Such a gap would also increase the risk of developing a "separate military ethos." It is not at all clear that the benefits to be gained at such cost would be worthwhile. Much of the data on military performance suggests that in time of war, the conscript citizen-soldier, whose analog we are seeking in the all-volunteer force, was a better soldier than the volunteer on the average. And in peacetime, it has been the volunteers who have been overrepresented in military stockades.

An alternative approach, and the one we recommend, is to develop recruitment efforts designed to obtain a broader and more fully representative cross section of individuals among first termers and also among career personnel in the military. The primary advantages of such an approach is that it tends to avoid the problems and pitfalls mentioned above. An additional advantage is that extending recruiting efforts beyond the gung ho may help to attract larger numbers of our brightest and most ambitious young people to a period of military service.

How could the military services actually implement this approach of recruiting from the full spectrum of the nation's young men and women? Two strategies may be distinguished, and we recommend both to some extent. First, the extrinsic incentives to enlistment—those rewards or inducements which are not directly linked to actual performance in the work role—should be geared toward a wider range of individuals, especially those who have relatively high educational aspirations, abilities, and interests. We will say a good deal more about this approach in a moment.

The second strategy is to modify intrinsic characteristics of military work roles so as to make them more broadly attractive. Bowers and his colleagues have urged organizational improvements in the military that would include (*a*) more participative management practices, (*b*) reducing the amount and effects of bureaucracy, and (*c*) increasing opportunities for independence in personal lives. They have argued that such changes will not only make the military organization more attractive (Bowers, 1975), but also lead to greater effectiveness (Franklin and Drexler, 1976). We must add that there remain intrinsic characteristics in some military work roles that are unusually demanding and cannot be changed.

Returning to extrinsic incentives, perhaps the most obvious one when considering any work role, military or civilian, is financial payment. The higher the level of pay, the more attractive the work role is assumed to be. In discussions about the feasibility of converting to an all-volunteer force, primary attention was directed to increasing military salaries, and efforts were made to estimate exactly how much money would be required to induce enough men to enlist under volunteer conditions (U.S. President's Commission on an All-Volunteer Armed Force, 1970). The recent pay increases were a *necessary* condition for establishing an all-volunteer military force, but in our view the higher salaries do not constitute *sufficient* conditions. In some respects, the emphasis on pay increases may have led us to overlook other important incentives to military service, while at the same time greatly increasing the cost of maintaining a volunteer force and creating a threat to benefits that may be essential in maintaining military effectiveness.

Greater Emphasis on Educational Incentives

One type of extrinsic incentive which seems especially well suited to increasing the proportion of citizen-soldiers in an all-volunteer force consists of educational benefits which can be available to those who serve a tour of duty in the military. Although young men and women bound for college represent a group especially high in ability and ambition, military recruiting policy has, to a large degree, treated them as unlikely prospects (Binkin and Johnston, 1973). And in its recent report to the Army, the Opinion Research Corporation (1974, p. viii) advised that, "while college students do not express strong opposition any longer to the military as an institution, enlistment still does not appeal to them. Noncollege men remain the Army's major market." But in that same report it was noted that educators rate "interference with education" as a primary deterrent to military service, and feel that this drawback could be offset by greater emphasis on the GI Bill as a source of support for a college education. Some of our own research and writing has also stressed the value of increased emphasis on educational benefits as an important means of maintaining a broader balance in both ability and ideology among military recruits (Johnston and Bachman, 1972).

In sum, under present (early 1977) conditions the typical high school student planning to attend college is likely to view military service as an unwise interruption of his educational development. Given no change in present conditions, or worse yet, given further reductions in educational benefits for veterans, it is probably quite accurate to conclude that noncollege men will remain the primary source of military personnel. But we think it would be unwise to leave present conditions as they are. On the contrary, we recommend that the educational benefits in return for military service be retained and enhanced, and that these benefits be publicized more widely. In particular, we would suggest the strengthening of pay-your-way-through-college plans that stress the opportunity to qualify for veterans' benefits, to amass substantial savings, and to accumulate some college credits during a tour of military service following high school. And to the extent that problems of broad representativeness are most severe in the ground combat branches of the armed forces, we see no reason why such incentives should not be used *selectively* to attract personnel to these specific areas.

But why should the military seek out individuals who are likely to serve only one term and then go on to college as civilians? Why should it deliberately recruit those who have such a low likelihood of reenlistment? Some of the advantages in terms of high ability levels and broader perspectives have been noted above. These help to balance out the costs of higher turnover among those who enter the military in order to work their way through college. But it should be added that a considerable degree of this kind of turnover is necessary and desirable in an organization which has only limited positions of leadership at the top.

We should be careful not to confuse such turnover with the problem of high attrition *during first enlistments*. The armed forces are presently experiencing considerable difficulties with recruits who do not satisfactorily complete their first tour of duty, and this is appropriately treated as a serious problem. By way of contrast, however, we think that the military should treat high rates of turnover *after one complete tour of duty* as a sign of organizational success rather than failure. We agree with Friedman (1967) that some proportion of "in-and-outers" is desirable in the military services, and we view the use of educational incentives as a particularly effective means for ensuring this sort of turnover. A "college-education-in-exchange-for-military-service" formula is a means of attracting able and motivated individuals who can learn quickly, serve effectively for one full tour of duty, and then leave, making room for other fresh recruits.

The educational-incentive approach need not be limited to plans requiring that military service precede college. On the contrary, there would be substantial advantages for some young men and women to receive college support first and then enter the service. This would help meet military needs for skilled and educated personnel. Moreover, it seems likely that the broadening and liberalizing effects of higher education, plus the maturity of additional years, would make the college graduates less malleable, more confident and self-reliant, and better able to handle responsibilities than those recruited at an earlier stage of education and maturity.

We view the characteristics listed above as distinct advantages to the military services, but this viewpoint is not universally shared. Some military leaders have stated a preference for the young high school graduate rather than the older, cautious, more questioning college graduate. This brings us back to the fundamental question: Who ought to staff the military services? If our aim is to recruit only the "my country, right or wrong" type of person, then perhaps it would be just as well to avoid a greater emphasis on educational incentives. However, if we want at least some of our men and women in uniform to raise questions, disagree on occasion, and perhaps even refuse to follow orders that they hold to be contrary to conscience or international law, then educational incentives, particularly those involving college prior to military service, may be of great value.

It is gratifying that the idea of increased use of educational incentives, which was supported by our earlier work (Johnston and Bachman, 1972) and reinforced by the findings presented here, has also been put forward by Janowitz and Moskos (1974) as one of the approaches for reducing racial (and social class) imbalance in the military. It is fortunate indeed that educational incentives can potentially deal with these problems of race and class while at the same time helping to ensure, voluntarily, a mix of in-and-outers plus career personnel which is closer to a citizen force, not to an ideologically isolated career force.

The Unique Qualities of Military Service

While we aim for a military force that is as ideologically representative of the American people as possible, it is our assumption that some differences will remain due to the unique nature and mission of the military. The commitment of individuals to organizations is in large measure a function of the degree to which there is complementarity between organizational and individual needs. To the degree to which individuals, by behaving in ways supportive of an organization, fulfill their own needs, their commitment to the organization will be increased. Where this complementarity does not exist, their commitment will be minimized (Segal, 1977).

This relationship poses a potential problem for the military organization. Because of its unique social function—the legitimate management of violence—the military requires of its personnel a degree of commitment that differs from that required by most other modern organizations (Segal, 1975). Military personnel, unlike their civilian counterparts, enter into a contract of unlimited liability with their employer. They cannot unilaterally terminate their employment any time they wish (although the Anglo-American nations have been experimenting with voluntary discharge systems). They are subject to moving and working in any environment in which the service decides they are needed. They are required to place the needs of the service above the needs of their families, and must frequently endure long periods of separation from their loved ones. They are frequently called upon to work more than an eight-hour day, for which they receive no additional compensation. And in time of war, they may face prolonged danger, and even death. Obviously, the commitment made by the man on the firing line is different from that made by the worker on the assembly line.

There has been considerable debate on whether the military can structurally resemble other organizations in modern society and still fulfill its combat function (Moskos, 1973a; Segal et al., 1974). There is an inherent strain between organizational requirements to maintain combat effectiveness, on the one hand, and societal pressures to maintain a socially representative and responsive military establishment, on the other. To the degree that military organization *must* differ from civilian organization in its structure and processes, it is likely to differ as well in its ability to fulfill individual needs insofar as the values of personnel within the military are similar to those of civilians.

The Convergence Theme

Military sociology in the 1950s and early 1960s suggested that military organization was becoming increasingly similar to industrial organization (Lang, 1964; Grusky, 1964). By the late 1960s and early 1970s, however, scholars were beginning to see limits to the degree to which structural convergence could occur (Janowitz, 1971). Moskos (1973a), for example, moved from a "convergence" position to posit a "segmented" model of the military in which combat formations diverge structurally from civilian institutions, while noncombat agencies converge.

Some analysts take as dogma the assumption that military organization, or some subsets of it, must be authoritarian, hierarchical, disciplined, and austere. Hauser (1973), for example, feels this is true for the combat formations of the Army. Recognizing that these are not the values that are emphasized in the mainstream of contemporary American life, he feels that convergence must be prevented. He envisages the American Army of the future as consisting of (*a*) combat formations that are kept relatively isolated from the civilian sector of society and thus protected from some of the turbulent processes in the civilian world (such as racial tension, drug abuse, and lack of discipline) and (*b*) a supporting Army which is in contact with civilian society and serves as a buffer between that society and its combat forces. Only in this way is an authoritarian force seen as surviving in a libertarian society.

The view that the military must be structurally different from other enterprises and insulated from them to retain that differential is, of course, not unique to Hauser. Huntington (1957) takes this same stance with regard to the conditions necessary for the maintenance of civilian control over the military. Other theorists, as we have noted earlier, take an opposite view. For example, although Janowitz (1973) feels that military and civilian organizational forms cannot converge completely, he sees social isolation of the military as a threat to civilian control of the military and indeed to the social legitimacy of the military institution. He believes that in order to maintain the viability of the American military, the boundary between military and civilian sectors of society must be permeable, and the personnel within the military must be broadly representative of the population of the civilian sector.

In sum, the goals of extensive civil-military contact and social representativeness of the forces can be seen as functional in the sense that they minimize the ideological distance between civilian and military sectors and mitigate against the development of a "military mind" within the armed forces. However, to the degree that some military work roles are quite different from most civilian work roles, there is the danger of a poor fit between individual needs and organizational needs; and that poor fit could have negative consequences for both the individuals and the military organization. Perhaps one of the ways of recognizing and dealing with this problem is to treat such military roles as a calling rather than just another occupation.

Military Service: A Calling or an Occupation?

Historically, the military has been structurally very different from civilian industrial organizations. Many jobs in the military did not have counterparts in the civilian labor force. The world of work was not distinct from the world of leisure: both worlds were integrated on the military installation, where personnel played, worked, shopped, and lived. The organization of work was communal, or fraternal, rather than industrial (Coates and Pellegrin, 1965).

Moskos (1976) has pointed out that in characterizing the military, the concepts of *profession, calling,* and *occupation* have been used in various circumstances. The model of a profession, applying at best only to the officer corps, implies legitimation through expertise based upon specialized training, certification as a professional, occupational autonomy, and a service orientation. This set of characteristics differentiates the profession from other occupational groups. While career officers have been regarded as professionals, this status has never been accorded to the junior enlisted ranks, and only rarely to senior noncommissioned officers. And the argument that the officer corps no longer comprises a profession in Britain, advanced by Abrams (1965), may also be applicable to the U.S. forces.

The concept of a calling suggests voluntarism and thus excludes conscripts. But a calling does not necessarily involve training and expertise, and thus is not restricted to officers. It does imply a sacred mission, legitimation through institutional values, a high level of devotion to the tasks of office, communion with others in the calling, and a reward system based not as much on salary as on a life-style

appropriate to the social position of the calling, i.e., on def-
erence rather than remuneration.

While military sociologists have repeatedly suggested
that the primary motivations in actual combat situations are
not ideological (e.g., Shils and Janowitz, 1948), structurally
the model of a calling has not been inappropriate for volunteers in the U.S. armed forces in years past. The mission of
the soldier was to defend his country, as sacred a mission as
a secular institution could perform. Indeed, military service
came to be a hallmark of participation in the democratic
polity in the Western world (Janowitz, 1975).

As noted above, the basic organization of the Army was
fraternal and communal. And the system of compensation
was defined not so much in terms of salary—indeed, military pay was rather low. Rather, the reward system was
defined in terms of (*a*) status differentiated life-styles (size
of military housing units vary by rank, for example) and (*b*)
manifestations of social honor, such as medals and parades.
It was characteristics such as these that differentiated the
calling of military service from industrial and commercial
occupations in the civilian sector whose legitimacy is based
upon a direct exchange of labor for wages. Of equal importance, whereas civilian wages are based on an explicit con-
tractual relationship specifying work to be done and compensation (including fringe benefits) to be received, the
compensation of military personnel, while defined at any
specific point in time by statute, has been rooted in an implied contract. This contract, on the basis of norm rather
than law, suggested (*a*) the indefinite continuation of personal and family benefits including health care, access to
commissaries and post exchanges, housing facilities or allowances, and (*b*) an understanding that once an initial period
of service had been successfully completed, and unless the
individual committed a major offense, retention was guar-
anteed until eligibility for a pension was reached at the end
of twenty years of service.

Three interrelated trends, related to the decline of the
mass armed force, are transforming the calling of military

service into a secular occupation. The first is a changing technology of warfare that makes civilian populations as vulnerable to attack as frontline troops, and thus has socialized the danger of war and reduced the unique liability and sacrifice of armed forces personnel (Lasswell, 1941).

The second trend is related to the convergence theme discussed above. As the technology of warfare has become both more destructive and more complex, the nature (although not the distribution) of jobs in the military has come to approximate jobs in civilian enterprise (e.g. Biderman, 1967). Thus, at the same time that the unique liability of the military organization in time of war is decreasing, so is the uniqueness of the tasks performed within that organization.

The third trend is the growing tendency for makers of military personnel policy to treat soldiering as equivalent to a civilian job (Moskos, 1975). We noted in chapter 1 some of the ways in which the conditions of working for the armed forces as a uniformed member of the service have increasingly come to resemble the employment conditions of a civilian occupation. No doubt some of the specific changes which have occurred are likely to prove useful. But it seems to us that an overall policy of blurring the distinctions between military service and civilian employment is likely to be counterproductive in some important respects. In particular, we think that treating service in the armed forces as an occupation rather than a calling, that is, viewing it merely as "military employment," is in some respects antithetical to the citizen-soldier approach we have been advocating.

Citizen-Soldiers in Contrast to "Military Employees"

At first glance it seems paradoxical to argue that the "military employment" described above moves away from the concept of the citizen-soldier. After all, either one can be viewed as representing a kind of convergence between the military and civilian sectors. But convergence turns out to be a somewhat slippery concept, and we must not make the mistake of assuming that one kind of convergence is equivalent to, or even compatible with, another kind. If we look at the social forces likely to operate in the recruitment and retention of military personnel under the military employment approach, it should become clearer that it does not encourage the kind of citizen-soldier we have been discussing.

Treating service in the armed forces as little more than military employment is likely to have the following effects:

1. Like most civilian occupations, military employment will attract individuals from only a limited range of the total population, those who find the military work role and its extrinsic rewards more attractive than the civilian alternatives available to them.

2. The same factors which make military employment initially attractive to certain individuals are also likely to foster longer-term career interests in a military job. And this, of course, leads away from the planned turnover—the deliberate emphasis on "in-and-outers"—that we advocated earlier in this chapter.

3. Because of their career interests, military employees (like their career-oriented counterparts in many civilian organizations) are more likely to "do it the company way" and avoid actions which might put them at a disadvantage in the competition for advancement up the military career ladder.

4. The effects described above have a clear potential for a vicious cycle: (*a*) higher proportions of military recruits enter the service with career hopes; (*b*) because the positions at the top are limited, higher proportions of the career hopefuls are going to be disappointed; (*c*) accordingly, competition for the limited advancement positions will become more severe; (*d*) and that in turn is likely to create even stronger pressures to conform to the military way.

There is nothing about the above analysis that is necessarily unique to the military. The dynamics described above for the military often operate in civilian organizations, particularly large-scale corporations with very hierarchical organizational structures. It could be argued that any such organization could benefit from having some proportion of its personnel be in-and-outers (individuals whose long-range plans lie elsewhere and who are therefore much freer to speak their minds).

While some proportion of in-and-outers would probably be good for many organizations, we think that the military is in some ways unique in its need for a substantial proportion of personnel who do *not* see their futures as lying within the organization, but instead see their fundamental interests and loyalties as lying elsewhere. Such citizen-soldiers might treat their single tour of military service as a "calling" in the sense discussed above. Hopefully, they would be intensely loyal to the nation and diligent in carrying out any missions assigned to them. But because they would not be anticipating military careers, they could more readily place the national interest (as, of course, they perceive it) ahead of their personal interests within the service.

As we have stated earlier, the concept of the citizen-soldier is not universally accepted. It involves some costs and complications for career military personnel. But, given the issues and findings summarized in this chapter, our own judgment is that a renewed emphasis upon the citizen-soldier is well worth the costs.

Is Conscription the Way to Guarantee Citizen-Soldiers?

Sooner or later, any discussion of the need for citizen-soldiers must deal with the possibility of a return to conscription. If we do not have a reasonably representative cross section of volunteers, and if we do not have a sufficient percentage of in-and-outers in the military, could we not overcome these problems simply by returning to the use of a military draft? Perhaps we could deal with these particular problems by reintroducing conscription, but we suspect that the other problems thereby created might make the cure much worse than the disease. In particular, a draft would be challenged on the basis of equity. The argument is that it is unfair to require a minority of the nation's youth to assume the burden and risks of military service while the majority of their age peers can avoid such service. This fundamental problem remains even if the draftees are selected by means of an impartial lottery. A solution, of course, is to require universal (or nearly universal) national service on the part of all young men and women. While such a massive mobilization of youth might have a number of advantages, it would be very difficult and expensive to employ, and thus seems unlikely.

In spite of issues of equity and the nation's basic distaste for compulsory service in anything less than a national emergency, some leaders in the military and Congress have recently come to look back longingly to the days when the draft could be counted upon to provide an adequate supply of personnel. Those were the days without all the worries about whether military salaries were equitable and whether young people understood and (in sufficient numbers) supported the nation's basic military policies. In particular, there has been a great temptation during a period of rising government costs and deficits to "cut military costs" by returning to conscription. There is no disputing the fact that if we were to return to conscription and drastically cut the pay levels for new recruits, we would reduce the *apparent* military personnel budget. But such an approach does not really save money, it simply redistributes the costs and hides them.

In any debate about the use of conscription to cut military costs, the real issue boils down to *who* should bear the costs of staffing the armed forces. As the Gates commission pointed out in 1970, a draft system which pays draftees (and draft-induced volunteers) less than would be required to induce truly voluntary service is actually a form of taxation—a "conscription tax."[1]

---

1. Indeed, the commission estimated that the conscription tax paid by draftees amounts to a tax burden more than three times that paid by comparable civilians. A commission staff report on the conscription tax put the matter succinctly: "As a tax, conscription under Selective Service is brutally inefficient—virtually in a class by itself." (Sjaastad and Hansen, 1970, p. IV–1–34)

Men who are forced to serve in the military at artificially low pay are actually paying a form of tax which subsidizes those in the society who do not serve.... This cost does not show up in the budget. Neither does the loss in output resulting from the disruption in the lives of young men who do not serve, but who rearrange their lives in response to the possibility of being drafted. Taking these hidden and neglected costs into account, the actual cost to the nation of an all-volunteer force will be lower than the cost of the present force. (U.S. President's Commission on an All-Volunteer Armed Force, 1970, p. 9)

This distinction between real costs and those which show up in a budget was not originated by the Gates commission. The point had been made at the 1966 University of Chicago conference on the draft by a number of participants, particularly economists Milton Freidman (1967) and Walter Oi (1967). Now, more than a decade later, we have had some experience with an all-volunteer force and we are indeed aware of the higher personnel budgets it involves. But we must not forget that a major reason for those higher budgets is the fact that we no longer levy a conscription tax on a small subset of the nation's youth. The costs of staffing our armed forces are now distributed across a broad range of taxpayers.

In sum, there is much room for honest disagreement about the wisdom of using some form of conscription as the means for ensuring citizen-soldiers or a socially balanced military. Our own view is that the role of citizen-soldier can better be restored within the all-volunteer framework; but given the nation's recent experience with the all-volunteer force (as noted in chapter 1), we can understand how others may be skeptical. However, we find ourselves much less tolerant of any argument that we should return to conscription as a means for reducing military personnel costs. It would be unconscionable to cut our military budgets by re-instituting the draft and then lowering military pay or benefits, for this would place heavy financial burdens on a small subset of our citizens at a time in their lives when most of them can least afford it. The fact that we used such a conscription tax in the past does not justify our doing so again, particularly now that we have had ample occasion to understand what is really involved.

Summary of Policy Implications

It seems to us that the debate about military personnel procurement in the all-volunteer force must be expanded across several dimensions. We need to open up the range of alternatives and move beyond both the economic incentive model on which the all-volunteer force was planned in the late sixties and the industrial model that was implemented in the middle seventies.

1. We need to think more about quality of military personnel and less about mere quantity. One of our major concerns about the *quality* of military personnel is to maintain and, indeed, strengthen the role of citizen-soldier within the all-volunteer force. This implies some balance with the civilian sector in terms of ideology, as well as ability, socioeconomic status, race, etc. It also implies a considerable proportion of individuals who consider their time in the service to be a relatively short-term activity, i.e., those who expect to make their careers in the civilian sector after a limited period of service in the armed forces. We emphasize, however, that the political role of the citizen-soldier is to balance, not to replace, the career military nucleus.

2. We need to expand the range of extrinsic incentives considered in recruitment (and retention) in the all-volunteer force. We should be more explicit about the *goals* of such efforts. For example, we may want to encourage a considerable proportion of in-and-outers to enter the armed forces in order to main-

tain a high proportion of citizen-soldiers. The methods we employ to reach our personnel goals should go beyond economic incentives, narrowly defined. Education and job training incentives, long a part of the military service package, need to be considered more explicitly and much more precisely as a part of the (extrinsic) incentive approach.

3. Finally, on the intrinsic incentive side—those things having to do with the military role itself—we need to develop a well-defined rationale for service. It may be well and good to stress higher pay rates, chances for training, and government contributions toward later civilian education, but these are all extrinsic incentives. If we are to have a wide cross section of viewpoints, of ideologies, recruited into the all-volunteer force, then the purpose of military service has to be presented in less vague terms than "serving your country." We need to develop a collective sense of the mission we expect our armed forces to fulfill in the international arena.

During the Second World War the rationale for service was compelling; the enemy was real and concrete and represented a great threat to the nation. Now, however, with Vietnam as the most recent example of military action, the problem is vastly more difficult. Many young people will not consider military service, no matter how attractive the extrinsic incentives, because they have questions about the legitimacy of the military and its mission.

Defining the mission of the U.S. armed forces is not something to be done by military leaders at the top levels, much less by those involved with military recruitment. There remains a need for an articulation of U.S. foreign policy as it might affect the use of military force. And that is a job for the civilian sector and the nation's leaders.

There are young men and women whose inclusion in the armed forces would strengthen it in terms of ability, ambition, demographic balance, and ideology. They are not the "my country, right or wrong" individuals. They are the ones who will support their country when they think it is right, and try to change it when they think it is wrong. Before a term of military service can be a legitimate possibility for them, i.e., before they can consider a tour of duty to be a "calling," there will have to be a clear and credible statement by the nation's leaders about those conditions under which we will, and will not, employ military force. As long as some of our youth perceive the use, or threat, of the instruments of mass destruction as simply another aspect of foreign policy to be used to maintain an advantaged position for this nation, they will remain unwilling to serve. Some of our best young people, including many who might greatly strengthen our armed forces, will not be "bought" no matter how attractive the extrinsic incentives. Before we can recruit these people as citizen-soldiers, we have to answer the question: For what?

Appendices

Description of Navy, Civilian, and Army Samples

A detailed description of sampling techniques as well as a description of the fit of the Navy and Civilian samples to their respective populations has been provided by Michaelsen (1973). A detailed description of the Army sample has been provided by Spencer (1975). The present descriptions have been excerpted from the Michaelsen and Spencer papers.

Navy Sample

Data from the Navy sample were collected from both ship and shore stations between November 1972 and February 1973. The questionnaires were personally administered by the Institute for Social Research personnel.

Ships were included from both the Atlantic and Pacific Fleets. Individuals in the sample were chosen in proportion to the number of personnel assigned to each ship type. For example, if 35 percent of the personnel assigned to ships were aboard destroyers, 35 percent of the individuals in the sample were selected so as to come from destroyers. Ships themselves were chosen largely on the basis of availability, with the specific ship selection occasionally influenced by the logistics of moving Organizational Research Program staff from one ship to another. As may be imagined, weather was also an occasional element in determining whether the necessary connections between two selected ships could be made.

For at least two reasons, an effort was made to maximize in the sample as many ships as possible currently deployed away from their home ports. First, larger proportions of the billets

163

are in fact filled on deployed ships than on ships in ports.
Second, personnel aboard deployed ships are more likely to have
had a period of exposure to the organizational variables being
measured. For these reasons, more than half of the ships
sampled were deployed at the time of the administration of the
survey.

Shore stations were included from eight shore station
commands (Atlantic Fleet, Pacific Fleet, Training, Material,
Personnel, Medicine and Surgery, Security, and Communications)
and from the CNO staff. Individuals in the sample were chosen
in proportion to the number of personnel assigned to each
command. Specific shore stations were randomly selected from
those available in four geographical areas--East Coast, Memphis-
Pensacola, San Diego, and Hawaii.

Personnel actually surveyed aboard a particular site were
members of intact organizational subunits, consisting of work
groups related to one another through supervisors who are, at
the same time, a superior of the group they supervise and a
subordinate in the group immediately above. In this fashion,
one may conceive of the organization as a structure of such
overlapping groups, a pyramid of interlaced pyramids. For purposes of identifying and selecting intact units for the study's
analytic aims, the sampling basis was designated as a "module,"
by which is meant a "pyramid" of groups three echelons tall.
Thus, members from four adjacent levels were included, with the
module head defined as the person at the apex of that particular three-tier pyramid. Yet another criterion for the selection
of a module was that the person at the apex (the module head)
had been at his current assignment for at least three months.

A list of all personnel at a site who met the criteria for
module head was obtained from manpower authorization documents
and from organizational charts, and from these rosters an appropriate number of module heads were randomly selected. If a
particular module did not provide a large enough sample of personnel required for the particular site, another module head
was selected by the same method. Thus, the sample from a site
consisted of one or more modules.

This sampling procedure resulted in data collection from 38
different Navy sites in a total sample size of 2522 Navy personnel.

Civilian Sample

The civilian data collection was conducted during February
and March of 1973, as part of a larger interview study conducted
by the Survey Research Center. The sample included 1327 dwelling
units, selected by a multistage sampling system so as to be representative of all dwellings in the coterminous United States
exclusive of those on military reservations.

At each housing unit, a trained interviewer from the Survey
Research Center conducted an interview with a specifically designated respondent, male or female, age 18 or older. The final
segment of the interview consisted of questions related to the
all-volunteer force. Following this personal interview, respondents were asked to complete the pencil-and-paper questionnaire.
In addition, copies of the questionnaire were administered to a
supplementary sample consisting of all other individuals age 16
or older who were present in each household at the time an interview was taken. Interviewers waited until all questionnaires in
a household were completed; none were left behind.

The 1327 interviews obtained represent a response rate of
75 percent. About 90 percent of those interviewed also filled
out questionnaires. These, plus the supplementary sample (those
who were not interviewed but did complete questionnaires), provided a total of about 1855 civilian questionnaires.

An examination of the interview sample and the supplementary sample, reported by Michaelsen (1973), showed no systematic
differences between the two, except for the fact that the supplementary sample included individuals aged 16 and 17. Because of
several advantages from a statistical standpoint, we have chosen
to treat the civilian interview and supplementary samples as a
single unweighted sample of people age 16 or older throughout
the United States.

Army Sample

A sample of 2286 Army officers and enlisted personnel was
drawn from a broad cross-section of units. The questionnaires
were personally administered by Institute for Social Research
personnel during a five month period between November 1974 and

April 1975.

Information necessary for sampling was gathered in the form
of data printouts which described the active Army in terms of
command structure, geographic location, size, function, and
mission.   The research plan required data from intact organizational units; therefore, it was necessary to identify organizational groupings which potentially included any individual in
the Army.   Since companies or battalions would not incorporate
all Army personnel, Parent Unit was designated as the primary
grouping for sampling purposes.

Once all Parent Units in the Army were listed, a total number could be obtained, a sampling frame determined, and every
"Nth" Parent Unit selected for inclusion in the sample.   However,
it was felt that representativeness could be enhanced by some
meaningful form of stratification.   After much exploration and
many trials, two strata were selected as appropriate and useful:
geographical location and functional designation (UNCLAC) of
each Parent Unit.

The study called for an Army sample of about 2500 respondents selected in such fashion as to include organizational units
at least three hierarchical levels tall.   These requirements
suggested a "module" (intact hierarchical set of groups) size of
approximately 50 respondents, and approximately 50 modules.

To select the 50 modules, two separate computer print-outs
were obtained containing all Parent Units in the Army.   One print-
out listed units by geographical location, while the second listed
them by functional designation of UNCLAC code. Based upon the
subtotals for major classifications within each of these print-
outs, the number of modules that should be drawn from each of
the major strata became evident.   Since the size of the project's
resources placed restrictions on the extent of data collection
that was feasible, it was decided to restrict the geographic
areas in which data collection would occur.   The requested and
obtained numbers of modules indicate that geographical representation was obtained:

Area	No. Modules Requested	No. Modules Obtained	Percent Obtained
Germany	15	12	80
Hawaii-Korea-Alaska	7	5	71
1st Army	10	7	70
5th Army	10	7	70
6th Army	6	6	100
Military District of Washington	2	0	0
TOTAL	50	37	76

A next step in selecting the sample was to obtain a list of Parent Units by UNCLAC, constrained on the above geographic locations. Finally there was needed some consideration for the size of the Parent Unit. The resulting sample would not be representative of the Army if large units and small units had an equal chance of being selected. Therefore, a weighting scheme was applied to all listed Parent Units, based upon the number of personnal in the unit. The weighting scheme was:

Number of Army Personnel in Parent Unit	Weight
0-49	0
50-149	1
150-249	2
250-349	3
350-449	4
450-549	5
etc.	etc.

The number of modules to be selected from a given UNCLAC classification was divided into the total number of Parent Unit weighting numbers. The result represented the sampling number to be used in conjunction with a random numbers table. For example, if a module was to be selected from a classification whose total weighting numbers added to 67, then a random numbers table would be used containing numbers from 1 to 67 and some predetermined one would be selected (the first number). If the first number were to be used, and it happened to be 16, then the Parent Units would be counted from the first to the sixteenth (according to the appropriate weighting numbers). The sixteenth Parent Unit would be selected for the sample.

Finally, the two stratifications -- geographic and functional -- were integrated. This was accomplished by creating a table with the geographic areas to be included and spaces for the number of units required for each. As Parent Units were selected, the table was completed.

Interrelationships among Military Values, Preferences, and Perceptions

In this appendix, we present some prior work (Bachman, 1974) which discusses the process of data reduction completed using the Navy and civilian samples. In addition, the appendix provides the details of the interpretation of the factor analysis and of the various measures. Appendix C gives the specifics on how the measures were constructed and which items were used.

The Measures of Values, Preferences and Perceptions

The questionnaire segment dealing with military values, preferences and perceptions (Section C) included 57 items, designed to measure a considerable number of different, but interrelated, concepts. These questionnaire items are reproduced in Appendix E. An important phase of our analysis involved the consolidation of these items into a smaller number of indexes. This data reduction effort served two purposes: first, it produced multi-item variables, which are generally more stable and reliable than single items; second, it reduced the complexity of the material to a more manageable level. A number of indexes had been constructed on an a priori basis; and some of these were presented in an earlier technical report (Bachman, 1973). Other indexes were planned, contingent upon finding that the items were satisfactorily intercorrelated. A few others were not anticipated in advance, but were developed out of our analysis of the intercorrelations among items.

An early stage in our efforts toward data reduction involved a number of preliminary factor analyses including nearly all of

169

the items in Section C of the questionnaire. These analyses confirmed most of our prior expectations about sets of variables to be combined into indexes; in a few other cases the analyses enabled us to locate items which did not meet our expectations.

It is not necessary for our present purposes to report the details of the preliminary analyses which led to further data reduction. It is worth noting, however, that these analyses were conducted separately for civilians, the Navy sample taken as a whole, and the three sub-groups within the Navy sample (officers, first-term enlisted men, later term enlisted men). The patterns of factors which emerged from these several groups were quite similar; thus we felt confident that the indexes we were developing were applicable across all the groups examined in this report.

Of the 57 items in the C section of the questionnaire, 42 were included in the set of 17 measures of values, preferences and perceptions used in our original analyses. Most of the measures are indexes based on two or more items, three one-item measures were included because they were conceptually important but did not lend themselves to combination into indexes. The listing of measures in Table 15 includes 15 of the 17 original measures. One of those measures, perceived discrimination against women and blacks, was not included in the analyses for the present volume (for reasons discussed in the text). Another measure, preference for higher military spending and influence, was modified (limited to spending only) in the present volume. Two measures were omitted from Table 15 in order to avoid an instance of redundancy. The indexes of perceived military influence and preferred military influence are the two ingredients for a single discrepancy measure (perceived minus preferred) which indicates the extent to which a respondent thinks the level of actual military influence exceeds, or falls short of, what he would consider ideal--thus we refer to that discrepancy measure as a measure of adequacy of military influence. In our final factor analyses the separate perceived and preferred measures were excluded, thus leaving a set of 15 measures in which each item appears no more than once.

A General Factor of Pro-Military Sentiment

Our earlier explorations of the data, and some examination
of the correlation matrices described above, led us to feel that
there is a "general factor" of pro-military (or anti-military)
sentiment underlying most of the measures we have been discussing.
In an effort to test this notion we performed a final set of
factor analyses.

As a first step, product-moment correlations were computed
among all of the measures in Table 15. The correlations were
computed for each of the following analysis groups separately:

> Navy first-term enlisted men
> Navy later-term enlisted men
> Navy officers
> Civilian men
> Civilian women

The complete correlation matrices are presented in Appendix B of
Bachman (1974). A bit later we will comment on selected portions
of the matrices, but first we turn to the factor analyses based
on them.

Our purpose in this series of factor analyses was not to
find a number of separate orthogonal factors (since that had
already been done in the earlier stages of analysis and index
development). Rather, we were looking for the largest and most
general single factor underlying the military value, preference
and perception measures. Accordingly, we used the principal
components method and focused attention on the first factor
(unrotated). The factor loadings for each of the five analysis
groups are displayed in the first five columns of Table 15.

The results shown in Table 15 clearly confirm our view that
there is a rather substantial general factor of "pro-military
sentiment" which contributes to our measures of military views.
It accounts for or "explains" between 23 percent and 30 percent
of the variance in these measures for Navy enlisted men and
civilians. (It accounts for 36 percent of the variance for Navy
officers, and the factor loadings for this group tend to be somewhat higher than is true for other groups. We will shortly consider a likely explanation for this pattern of stronger intercorrelations for the officer group.)

Table 15

Loadings on a General Factor of "Pro-Military Sentiment"*

	Navy sample			Civilian sample		
	1st-term enlisted (N=1194)	Later-term enlisted (N=834)	Officers (N=310)	Men (N=753)	Women (N=1053)	Male college graduates (N=113)
Perceived military job opportunities	.6088	.5830	.7212	.4225	.4030	.5271
Perceived fair treatment in services	.5727	.5665	.6997	.5015	.4982	.5469
Perceived competence of military leaders	.6909	.6491	.7739	.6661	.6924	.7198
Servicemen should obey without question	.5508	.5079	.4293	.5607	.5710	.5718
Should obey in My Lai-type situation	.5232	.3235	.3289	.5398	.4823	.6231
Support for military intervention	.4572	.4945	.5689	.4127	.2626	.5772
Preference for U.S. military supremacy	.5810	.4368	.6479	.6032	.5886	.6387
Support for U.S. actions in Vietnam	.7195	.6928	.7749	.6919	.6832	.7468
Role of military seen as positive	.5786	.3236	.5351	.5421	.5778	.6265
Preference for higher military spending & influence	.6542	.4486	.7707	.7270	.6951	.8466
Adequacy of military influence (Perc. minus Pref.)	-.5225	-.3295	-.6630	-.6274	-.5149	-.7402
Preference for "citizen soldiers"	-.0804	-.3197	-.4203	-.1301	-.1203	-.2379
Preference for wide range of views among servicemen	-.0854	-.2852	-.3019	-.3515	-.2025	-.5133
Support for amnesty	-.5855	-.6045	-.7273	-.6464	-.6067	-.7566
Perceived discrimination against women and blacks	-.2142	-.3715	-.4677	-.3996	-.3772	-.5856
Variance explained (by first factor)	28.4%	23.1%	36.1%	29.5%	26.5%	40.1%

*Table entries are loadings on the first factor (unrotated) using the principal components method.

There is a considerable degree of similarity in the patterns
of factor loadings for all five analysis groups. Without exception, the direction of loading is the same for all analysis
groups--i.e., a measure is either positively loaded for all
groups or negatively loaded for all. Moreover, those measures
which load most strongly are the same across all groups.

Let us consider what it means to be high in our general
factor of pro-military sentiment. Not surprisingly, those highest in pro-military sentiment rate our military leaders as quite
competent, give the military services high marks for job opportunity and fair treatment, state a preference for higher levels
of military spending and influence, and see the role of the military in society as predominantly positive. Their foreign
policy views are rather "hawkish"--they are relatively supportive
of U.S. military intervention in other countries, they prefer a
position of military supremacy (rather than parity with the
U.S.S.R.), they are most likely to support past U.S. involvement
in Vietnam, and they are strongly opposed to amnesty for those
who refused to serve in Vietnam. Finally, they place a high
value on obedience to military authority--they tend to agree that
"servicemen should obey orders without question" and some
maintain this position even when faced with a My Lai-type incident.

Among all the dimensions summarized above, the measure of
support for U.S. actions in Vietnam has a particularly strong
loading on the general factor of military sentiment. One possible
interpretation for this relationship is that those who are generally supportive of the military establishment have, as a result,
been least critical of our past involvement in Vietnam. In other
words, Vietnam views are shaped by broader attitudes about the
military. An alternative interpretation is that views about the
Vietnam involvement are generalized to the larger military
establishment, so that negative feelings about Vietnam lead to
negative views about military spending, influence, leadership,
and the like. These two interpretations are not mutually
exclusive--indeed, it is likely that both patterns of causation
are at work. But it is surely worth emphasizing that, as of
early 1973, feelings about Vietnam were a very central ingredient in overall sentiment toward the military services.

The measures which show little association with the general
factor of military sentiment are the dimensions most closely
linked to the debate about the draft versus the all-volunteer
force--preference for citizen soldiers and preference for wide
range of political views among servicemen.   These two dimensions
seem to stand somewhat apart from most of the other measures and
are less integrated into an overall pro-military or anti-military
continuum.   It is perhaps worth noting that the rather small
loadings for these dimensions are in a negative direction, suggesting that those with the most favorable feelings toward the military services are a bit less likely to prefer citizen soldiers
or a wide range of political views among servicemen.   Nevertheless, our more basic conclusion is that our respondents show
little polarization along these dimensions--perhaps indicating
that most people have not given much thought to the issues they
represent.

Up to this point we have been concentrating upon relationships which are consistent across the several Navy and civilian
analysis groups.   Now let us turn to some interesting differences
among these groups.   We noted in an early report (Bachman, 1973)
that the measure of military job opportunity is a stronger correlate of pro- or anti-enlistment views among Navy men than among
civilians.   In the present factor analyses we see a parallel tendency reflected in the higher factor loadings for military job
opportunity among each of the three Navy groups.   A similar
pattern, though not so strong, appears for the measure of perceived fair treatment in the services.   It seems quite reasonable
that military job opportunities and fair treatment would play a
relatively large part in the overall military sentiment of those
presently in the Navy; it is interesting also to note that the
finding is fully as strong for officers as for enlisted men.

Another difference of interest is one mentioned earlier--the
tendency for Navy officers to show generally stronger correlation
than do the other Navy or civilian groups.   These stronger correlations can be observed in Appendix B in Bachman (1974), and
they are also reflected in the factor analysis loadings and
explained variance shown in Table 15.   When we first became aware
of this pattern of stronger relationships for Navy officers, we
thought it might reflect their deep personal involvement and the

fact that they, more than civilians or enlisted men, have thought about the issues treated here and tried to place them in a consistent perspective.

But it also occurred to us that consistency in questionnaire responses is sometimes related to intelligence or education. Since the great majority of Navy officers are college graduates, it seemed quite possible that the pattern of relatively stronger correlations among officers is simply due to their higher average level of education. This suspicion was confirmed when we compared Navy officers with the subgroup of civilian men who had completed college (N=133). The results of the factor analysis for this group, presented in the last column of Table 15, show a striking similarity to the results for Navy officers in overall strength of relationships. A few differences may be noted: factor loadings for perceived military job opportunities and perceived fair treatment in services remain higher for the Navy officers than for the civilian college graduates, whereas factor loadings for the obedience items are relatively higher for the civilian group. On the whole, however, the two groups show rather similar patterns of relationships, and this leads us to conclude that the high pattern of correlations among Navy officers is more a reflection of their education than their special interest in the topics covered.

Item Ingredients for Military Value, Preference, and Perception Measures

This appendix displays each major measure (underlined) along with its item(s) listed by question number. The response scale for each item is indicated by its end points, and the scoring shown is that used to construct the measure. Those items marked with an "R" had to be recoded in reverse for index purposes; in such cases the response scale shown in this table is the recoded (reversed) version. Unless otherwise indicated, indexes are means of the items shown, with no missing data allowed.

Perceived Military Job Opportunities

All items share the following introduction:
To what extent to you think the following opportunities are available to people who work in the military services: (1=very little extent; 5=very great extent)

C1. A chance to get ahead
C2. A chance to get more education
C3. A chance to advance to a more responsible position
C4. A chance to have a personally more fulfilling job
C5. A chance to get their ideas heard
(One item of missing data allowed in index construction.)

Perceived Fair Treatment in Service

C6. To what extent is it likely that a person in the military can get things changed and set right if he is being treated unjustly by a superior? (1=very little extent; 5=very great extent)
C9R. Do you personally feel that you would receive more just and fair treatment as a civilian or as a member of the military service? (Reversed: 1=much more fair as civilian; 5=much more fair in service; 6, "question not appropriate for me" treated as missing data)

Perceived Competence of Military Leaders

C19. To what extent do you think our military leaders are smart people who know what they are doing? (1=very little extent; 5=very great extent)
C24. To what extent do you think you can trust our military leadership to do what is right? (1=very little extent; 5=very great extent)

176

Servicemen Should Obey Without Question

C53R.   Servicemen should obey orders without question.
(Reversed: 1=disagree; 4=agree)

Should Obey in My Lai-Type Situation

C54R.   Suppose a group of soldiers in Vietnam were ordered by their superior officers to shoot all inhabitants of a village suspected of aiding the enemy including old men, women and children? In your opinion, what should the soldiers do in such a situation? *(Reversed: 1=refuse to shoot them; 2=don't know; 3=follow orders and shoot)*

Support for Military Intervention

C39R.   There may be times when the U.S. should go to war to protect the rights of other countries. (Reversed: 1=disagree; 4=agree)

C41.   The only good reason for the U.S. to go to war is to defend against an attact on our own country. (1=agree; 4=disagree)

Preference for U.S. Military Supremacy

C42.   The U.S. does not need to have greater military power than the Soviet Union. (1=agree; 4=disagree)

C43R.   The U.S. ought to have much more military power than any other nation in the world. (1=disagree; 4=agree)

Support for U.S. Action in Vietnam

C45.   Fighting the war in Vietnam has been damaging to our national honor or pride. (1=agree; 4=disagree)

C46.   Fighting the war in Vietnam has not really been in the national interest. (1=agree; 4=disagree)

C47R.   Fighting the war in Vietnam has been important to fight the spread of Communism. (Reversed: 1=disagree; 4=agree)

C48.   Fighting the war in Vietnam has brought us closer to world war. (1=agree; 4=disagree)

C49R.   Fighting the war in Vietnam has been important to protect friendly countries. (Reversed: 1=disagree; 4=agree)

C50R.   Fighting the war in Vietnam has been important to show other nations that we keep our promises.
(One item of missing data allowed in index construction.)

Role of Military Seen as Positive

C27R.   Overall, how do you feel about the role of the military services in our society during the time since World War II--has it been mostly positive or mostly negative? (Reversed: 1=strongly negative; 4=strongly positive)

Preference for Higher Military Spending

C26.   Do you think the U.S. spends too much or too little on the armed services? (1=far too much; 5=far too little)

Perceived Military (Versus Civilian) Influence

C28. Who has most influence over whether to involve U.S. servicemen in foreign conflicts? (see note below)

C30. Who has most influence over what tactics to use on the battlefield?

C32. Who has most influence over which new weapon systems to develop?

C34. Who has most influence over levels of pay and fringe benefits in the armed services?

C36. Who has most influence over whether to use nuclear weapons?

Each question above is followed by the statement: "This is how I think it is now:" (1=civilians much more; 5=military much more)
(One item of missing data allowed in index construction.)

Preferred Military (Versus Civilian) Influence

C29, C31, C33, C35, C37
The questions are the same as C28 through C36 above, with each question followed by the statement: "This is how I'd like it to be:" (1=civilians much more; 5=military much more)
(One item of missing data allowed in index construction.)

Adequacy of Military Influence (Perceived Minus Preferred)

This measure consists of the discrepancy or difference between the two indexes above. Specifically, the measure is computed as follows:

$$\text{Adequacy of Military Influence} = \left(\begin{array}{c}\text{Perceived}\\\text{Influence}\end{array}\right) - \left(\begin{array}{c}\text{Preferred}\\\text{Influence}\end{array}\right) + 4$$

The constant 4 is added to avoid negative numbers. A score on this measure larger than 4 indicates that perceived military influence is greater (more "adequate") than the respondent would prefer; a score lower than 4 indicates the reverse--military influence less adequate than the respondent would prefer.

Preference for "Citizen Soldiers" (Versus "Career Men")

C12R. Most of our servicemen should be "citizen soldiers"--men who spend just three or four years in the military and then return to civilian life. (Reversed: 1=disagree; 4=agree)

C13. Our military service should be staffed mostly with "career men" who spend twenty or more years in the service. (1=agree; 4=disagree)

Preferred Wide Range of Political Views Among Servicemen

C14. Only those who agree with our military policy should be allowed to serve in the armed forces. (1=agree; 4=disagree)

C15R. There ought to be a wide range of different political viewpoints among those in the military service. (Reversed: 1=disagree; 4=agree)

Support for Amnesty

C51. Going to Canada to avoid fighting in Vietnam was wrong, and those who did so should be punished. (1=agree; 4=disagree)

C52R. The men who went to Canada rather than fight in Vietnam were doing what they felt was right. They should be allowed to return to the U.S. without being punished. (Reversed: 1=disagree; 4=agree)

Supplementary Tables

Table 16

Scale Midpoints and Scores for All Civilians

	a. Scale Midpoints	b. Mean Scores	c. Standard Deviations	d. "Pro-Military" Deviation Score*
Perceived military job opportunities	3	3.40	.89	+.45
Perceived fair treatment in services	3	2.47	.87	-.61
Perceived competence of military leaders	3	3.39	.92	+.42
Servicemen should obey without question	2.5	2.80	.97	+.31
Should obey in My Lai-type situation	2	1.83	.74	-.23
Support for military intervention	2.5	2.24	.79	-.33
Preference for U.S. military supremacy	2.5	2.85	.88	+.40
Support for U.S. actions in Vietnam	2.5	2.54	.72	+.06
Role of military seen as positive	2.5	2.72	.67	+.33
Preference for higher military spending	3	2.60	.89	-.45
Perceived military (vs. civilian) influence	3	3.20	1.06	-.19*
Preferred military (vs. civilian) influence	3	3.18	.83	+.22
Adequacy of military influence (perc.-pref.)	4	4.02	1.30	-.02*
Preference for "citizen soldiers"	2.5	2.59	.85	-.11*
Preferred wide range of views among servicemen	2.5	2.78	.81	-.35*
Support for amnesty	2.5	2.05	1.09	+.41*

*The deviation score is computed using data from columns a, b, and c according to the following formula: $\frac{b-a}{c}$
For the five dimensions marked with an asterisk, the signs are reversed because they correlate negatively with "pro-military" sentiment.

Table 17

Mean Scores for Civilian Groups by Age and Education

	Younger (≤34)		Older (≥35)	
	College Grads (N=116)	Non-Grads (N=645)	College Grads (N=128)	Non-Grads (N=836)
Perceived military job opportunities	3.02	3.39	3.20	3.47
Perceived fair treatment in services	2.01	2.48	2.25	2.57
Perceived competence of military leaders	2.95	3.27	3.35	3.56
Servicemen should obey without question	2.16	2.58	2.82	3.09
Should obey in My Lai-type situation	1.47	1.80	1.76	1.92
Support for military intervention	2.24	2.29	2.30	2.20
Preference for U.S. military supremacy	2.29	2.76	2.58	3.04
Support for U.S. actions in Vietnam	2.15	2.51	2.45	2.64
Role of military seen as positive	2.45	2.68	2.66	2.80
Preference for higher military spending	2.03	2.60	2.39	2.71
Perceived military (vs. civilian) influence	3.34	3.37	2.95	3.08
Preferred military (vs. civilian) influence	2.83	3.12	2.83	3.34
Adequacy of military influence (perc.-pref.)	4.51	4.25	4.12	3.74
Preference for "citizen soldiers"	2.68	2.69	2.25	2.53
Preferred wide range of views among servicemen	3.11	2.81	2.89	2.70
Support for amnesty	2.63	2.28	2.01	1.79

Table 18

Mean Scores for Career and Non-Career Enlisted Groups

	Non-Career		Career	
	Navy (N=1134)	Army (N=887)	Navy (N=867)	Army (N=934)
Perceived military job opportunities	2.97	3.01	3.76	3.84
Perceived fair treatment in services	1.97	2.15	3.00	3.15
Perceived competence of military leaders	2.65	2.55	3.50	3.28
Servicemen should obey without question	2.17	2.07	2.93	2.68
Should obey in My Lai-type situation	1.77	1.72	2.03	1.83
Support for military intervention	2.25	2.20	2.81	2.63
Preference for U.S. military supremacy	2.68	2.85	3.20	3.27
Support for U.S. actions in Vietnam	2.32	2.34	2.84	2.74
Role of military seen as positive	2.55	2.48	2.86	2.75
Preference for higher military spending	2.97	3.19	3.62	3.84
Perceived military (vs. civilian) influence	2.93	2.89	2.15	2.33
Preferred military (vs. civilian) influence	3.29	3.56	3.71	4.04
Adequacy of military influence (perc.-pref.)	3.64	3.33	2.44	2.29
Preference for "citizen soldiers"	2.64	2.71	2.16	2.14
Preferred wide range of views among servicemen	2.78	2.81	2.75	2.74
Support for amnesty	2.54	2.52	1.53	1.66

183

Table 19

Mean Scores for Career and Non-Career Officer Groups

	Non-Career		Career	
	Navy (N=85)	Army (N=45)	Navy (N=223)	Army (N=194)
Perceived military job opportunities	2.92	3.48	3.91	3.92
Perceived fair treatment in services	2.34	2.88	3.26	3.27
Perceived competence of military leaders	2.89	3.52	3.82	3.81
Servicemen should obey without question	2.59	2.42	2.77	2.61
Should obey in My Lai-type situation	1.44	1.38	1.60	1.27
Support for military intervention	2.40	2.77	2.93	3.08
Preference for U.S. military supremacy	2.32	2.83	2.87	2.94
Support for U.S. actions in Vietnam	2.00	2.54	2.69	2.77
Role of military seen as positive	2.52	2.78	2.93	2.86
Preference for higher military spending	2.31	3.42	3.27	3.71
Perceived military (vs. civilian) influence	2.45	2.17	1.98	1.93
Preferred military (vs. civilian) influence	2.77	3.36	3.14	3.50
Adequacy of military influence (perc.-pref.)	3.68	2.81	2.83	2.43
Preference for "citizen soldiers"	2.54	2.62	2.06	2.10
Preferred wide range of views among servicemen	2.89	3.21	3.07	3.06
Support for amnesty	2.22	1.68	1.43	1.47

184

Table 20

Mean Scores for Civilian Comparison Groups

	Youth age 19-24 (N=249)	Non-College Graduates (weighted)	Younger Coll. Grads (N=116)	All College Graduates (N=242)
Perceived military job opportunities	3.38	3.42	3.02	3.12
Perceived fair treatment in services	2.38	2.51	2.01	2.13
Perceived competence of military leaders	3.07	3.37	2.95	3.16
Servicemen should obey without question	2.34	2.75	2.16	2.50
Should obey in My Lai-type situation	1.68	1.84	1.47	1.62
Support for military intervention	2.20	2.26	2.24	2.28
Preference for U.S. military supremacy	2.57	2.85	2.29	2.44
Support for U.S. actions in Vietnam	2.36	2.56	2.15	2.30
Role of military seen as positive	2.47	2.72	2.45	2.56
Preference for higher military spending	2.48	2.64	2.03	2.22
Perceived military (vs. civilian) influence	3.52	3.27	3.34	3.13
Preferred military (vs. civilian) influence	3.06	3.20	2.83	2.83
Adequacy of military influence (perc.-pref.)	4.46	4.08	4.51	4.30
Preference for "citizen soldiers"	2.72	2.64	2.68	2.46
Preferred wide range of views among servicemen	2.89	2.77	3.11	3.00
Support for amnesty	2.61	2.11	2.63	2.30

Table 21

Mean Scores on Military Versus Civilian Influence Items for Civilian Groups by Age and Education

	All Civilians (N=1677)	Younger (≤ 34)		Older (≥35)	
		Coll. Grads (N=113)	Non-Grads (N=640)	Coll. Grads (N=127)	Non-Grads (N=797)
Battlefield tactics					
Perceived	(3.91)	4.25	4.00	3.80	3.82
Preferred	(3.93)	3.85	3.82	3.88	4.04
Choice of new weapons					
Perceived	(3.46)	3.78	3.60	3.40	3.30
Preferred	(3.44)	3.06	3.35	3.17	3.62
Military pay levels					
Perceived	(2.77)	2.82	2.94	2.48	2.69
Preferred	(3.02)	2.83	3.01	2.62	3.12
Foreign involvements					
Perceived	(2.96)	3.15	3.12	2.72	2.83
Preferred	(2.68)	2.16	2.66	2.20	2.85
Nuclear weapons use					
Perceived	(2.90)	2.73	3.19	2.37	2.77
Preferred	(2.85)	2.27	2.80	2.30	3.05

Table 22

Mean Scores on Military vs. Civilian Influence Items for Navy Groups by Career-Orientation and Rank

	Total Navy	Non-Career Oriented		Career Oriented	
		Officers (N=86)	Enlisted Men (N=1133)	Officers (N=223)	Enlisted Men (N=874)
Battlefield tactics					
Perceived	(3.42)	3.45	3.88	2.83	2.97
Preferred	(4.36)	4.06	4.22	4.58	4.51
Choice of new weapons					
Perceived	(2.78)	3.23	3.15	2.58	2.32
Preferred	(3.77)	3.36	3.57	3.90	4.05
Military pay levels					
Perceived	(2.01)	1.74	2.35	1.63	1.69
Preferred	(3.44)	2.71	3.28	3.09	3.81
Foreign involvements					
Perceived	(2.35)	2.14	2.79	1.60	2.00
Preferred	(2.80)	2.02	2.66	2.25	3.20
Nuclear weapons use					
Perceived	(2.07)	1.70	2.51	1.22	1.76
Preferred	(2.70)	1.70	2.73	1.88	2.98

Table 23

Mean Scores on Military vs. Civilian Influence Items for Army Groups by Career-Orientation and Rank

	Total Navy	Non-Career Oriented		Career Oriented	
		Officers (N=45)	Enlisted Men (N=899)	Officers (N=193)	Enlisted Men (N=932)
Battlefield tactics					
Perceived	(3.59)	3.62	3.85	3.30	3.41
Preferred	(4.50)	4.67	4.27	4.69	4.67
Choice of new weapons					
Perceived	(2.68)	2.44	3.03	2.23	2.44
Preferred	(4.03)	3.93	3.78	4.04	4.28
Military pay levels					
Perceived	(2.03)	1.51	2.39	1.38	1.84
Preferred	(3.76)	3.40	3.55	3.39	4.07
Foreign involvement					
Perceived	(2.17)	1.80	2.54	1.40	1.99
Preferred	(3.22)	2.47	2.95	2.77	3.61
Nuclear weapons use					
Perceived	(2.20)	1.47	2.65	1.34	1.98
Preferred	(3.31)	2.31	3.23	2.58	3.57

Part C of Questionnaire:
Opinions about the Military Services

PART C

These next questions ask for your opinions about the military services in the United States. Some questions ask about the way you think things actually are, and others ask about the way you would like things to be.

To what extent do you think the following opportunities are available to people who work in the military services?	To a very little extent	To a little extent	To some extent	To a great extent	To a very great extent
1. A chance to get ahead	①	②	③	④	⑤
2. A chance to get more education	①	②	③	④	⑤
3. A chance to advance to a more responsible position	①	②	③	④	⑤
4. A chance to have a personally more fulfilling job	①	②	③	④	⑤
5. A chance to get their ideas heard	①	②	③	④	⑤

6. To what extent is it likely that a person in the military can get things changed and set right if he is being treated unjustly by a superior?
① ② ③ ④ ⑤

7. To what extent do you think there is any discrimination against women who are in the armed services?
① ② ③ ④ ⑤

8. To what extent do you think there is any discrimination against black people who are in the armed services?
① ② ③ ④ ⑤

9. Do you personally feel that <u>you</u> would receive more just and fair treatment as a civilian or as a member of the military service?
 ① Much more fair in the military service
 ② More fair in the military service
 ③ About the same
 ④ More fair as a civilian
 ⑤ Much more fair as a civilian
 ⑥ Question not appropriate for me

10. If you had a son in his late teens or early twenties who decided to enter the military service, how would you feel about his decision?
 ① Strongly positive
 ② Mostly positive
 ③ Mostly negative
 ④ Strongly negative

	Agree	Agree Mostly	Disagree Mostly	Disagree
11. The United States should provide high enough salaries and benefits so that it can man its armed forces with volunteers.	①	②	③	④
12. Most of our servicemen should be "citizen soldiers" – men who spend just three or four years in the military and then return to civilian life.	①	②	③	④
13. Our military service should be staffed mostly with "career men" who spend twenty or more years in the service.	①	②	③	④
14. Only those who agree with our military policy should be allowed to serve in the armed forces.	①	②	③	④
15. There ought to be a wide range of different political viewpoints among those in the military service.	①	②	③	④

189

16. In some countries the military forces have taken over and thrown out the civilian government. Do you think there is any chance that this could happen in the United States?

①It probably will happen in the U. S.

②It is certainly possible, but not very likely.

③It is nearly impossible.

④It could never happen in the U. S.

17. To what extent do you think our armed forces are capable of meeting all of our present military needs?

	To a very little extent	To a little extent	To some extent	To a great extent	To a very great extent
	①	②	③	④	⑤

18. To what extent do you think the military makes efficient use of the money in its budget?

| ① | ② | ③ | ④ | ⑤ |

19. To what extent do you think our military leaders are smart people who know what they are doing?

| ① | ② | ③ | ④ | ⑤ |

20. To what extent would it be possible to improve the caliber of our officer ranks?

| ① | ② | ③ | ④ | ⑤ |

21. To what extent do we fall, short of the military preparedness we need in today's world?

| ① | ② | ③ | ④ | ⑤ |

22. To what extent is there waste in the way our military services are run at present?

| ① | ② | ③ | ④ | ⑤ |

23. To what extent do you think military officers try to do as good a job as they can?

| ① | ② | ③ | ④ | ⑤ |

24. To what extent do you think you can trust our military leadership to do what is right?

| ① | ② | ③ | ④ | ⑤ |

25. All things considered, do you think the armed services presently have too much or too little influence on the way this country is run?

① Far too much

② Too much

③ About right

④ Too little

⑤ Far too little

26. Do you think the U. S. spends too much or too little on the armed services?

① Far too much

② Too much

③ About right

④ Too little

⑤ Far too little

27. Overall, how do you feel about the role of the military services in our society during the time since World War II – has it been mostly positive or mostly negative?

① Strongly Positive

② Mostly Positive

③ Mostly Negative

④ Strongly Negative

The next questions ask your opinion about the influence that military leaders and civilian leaders (such as the President or Congress) have over certain decisions affecting national security.

Who has most influence over whether to involve U. S. servicemen in foreign conflicts?

28. This is how I think it is now:

	Civilians much more	Civilians somewhat more	About equal influence	Military somewhat more	Military much more
	①	②	③	④	⑤

29. This is how I'd like it to be:

| ① | ② | ③ | ④ | ⑤ |

Who has most influence over what tactics to use on the battlefield?

30. This is how I think it is now:

① ② ③ ④ ⑤

31. This is how I'd like it to be:

① ② ③ ④ ⑤

Who has most influence over which new weapon systems to develop?

32. This is how I think it is now:

① ② ③ ④ ⑤

33. This is how I'd like it to be:

① ② ③ ④ ⑤

Who has most influence over levels of pay and fringe benefits in the armed services?

34. This is how I think it is now:

① ② ③ ④ ⑤

35. This is how I'd like it to be:

① ② ③ ④ ⑤

Who has most influence over whether to use nuclear weapons?

36. This is how I think it is now:

① ② ③ ④ ⑤

37. This is how I'd like it to be:

① ② ③ ④ ⑤

(Column headings for items 30–37: Civilians much more, Civilians somewhat more, About equal influence, Military somewhat more, Military much more)

(Column headings for items 38–40: Agree, Agree Mostly, Disagree Mostly, Disagree)

38. The U. S. should begin a gradual program of disarming whether other countries do or not.

① ② ③ ④

39. There may be times when the U. S. should go to war to protect the rights of other countries.

① ② ③ ④

40. The U. S. should be willing to go to war to protect its own economic interests.

① ② ③ ④

(Column headings for items 41–52: Agree, Agree Mostly, Disagree Mostly, Disagree)

41. The only good reason for the U. S. to go to war is to defend against an attack on our own country.

① ② ③ ④

42. The U. S. does not need to have greater military power than the Soviet Union.

① ② ③ ④

43. The U. S. ought to have much more military power than any other nation in the world.

① ② ③ ④

44. Our present foreign policy is based on our own narrow economic and power interests.

① ② ③ ④

45. Fighting the war in Vietnam has been damaging to our national honor or pride.

① ② ③ ④

46. Fighting the war in Vietnam has not really been in the national interest.

① ② ③ ④

47. Fighting the war in Vietnam has been important to fight the spread of Communism.

① ② ③ ④

48. Fighting the war in Vietnam has brought us closer to world war.

① ② ③ ④

49. Fighting the war in Vietnam has been important to protect friendly countries.

① ② ③ ④

50. Fighting the war in Vietnam has been important to show other nations that we keep our promises.

① ② ③ ④

51. Going to Canada to avoid fighting in Vietnam was wrong, and those who did so should be punished.

① ② ③ ④

52. The men who went to Canada rather than fight in Vietnam were doing what they felt was right. They should be allowed to return to the U. S. without being punished.

① ② ③ ④

	Agree	Agree Mostly	Disagree Mostly	Disagree

53. Servicemen should obey orders without question.
    ① ② ③ ④

54. Suppose a group of soldiers in Vietnam were ordered
    by their superior officers to shoot all inhabitants of a
    village suspected of aiding the enemy including old
    men, women and children? In your opinion, what
    should the soldiers do in such a situation?
    ① Follow orders and shoot

    ② Refuse to shoot them

    ③ Don't know

55. What do you think most people actually would do if
    they were in this situation?
    ① Follow orders and shoot

    ② Refuse to shoot them

    ③ Don't know

56. What do you think you would do in this situation?
    ① Follow orders and shoot

    ② Refuse to shoot them

    ③ Don't know

57. In general to what extent do your friends agree
    (disagree) with your views on the armed forces?
    ① Practically all agree

    ② Many agree

    ③ Some agree, some disagree

    ④ Many disagree

    ⑤ Practically all disagree

Bibliography

Abrahamsson, Bengt. "The Ideology of an Elite." In *Armed Forces and Society,* edited by Jacques Van Doorn. The Hague: Mouton, 1968.
———. *Military Professionalization and Political Power.* Beverly Hills: Sage Publications, 1972.
Abrams, Philip. "The Late Profession of Arms: Ambiguous Goals and Deteriorating Means in Britain." *European Journal of Sociology* 6 (1965): 238–61.
Angell, Robert C. "A Study of Social Values: Content Analysis of Elite Medias." *Journal of Conflict Resolution* 4 (1965): 329–85.
Assembly of Western European Union. "Conditions of Service in the Armed Forces." Document 650. Twentieth Ordinary Session. NATO report. November, 1974.
Bachman, Jerald G. "Values, Preferences and Perceptions Concerning Military Service." Ann Arbor: Institute for Social Research, 1973. (NTIS no. AD 763 483.)*
———. "Values, Preferences and Perceptions Concerning Military Service: Part II." Ann Arbor: Institute for Social Research, 1974. (NTIS no. AD 775 205.)*
Bachman, Jerald G., and Blair, John D. "Soldiers, Sailors, and Civilians: The 'Military Mind' and the All-Volunteer Force." Ann Arbor: Institute for Social Research, 1975. (NTIS no. AD A035 092.)*
———. " 'Citizen Force' or 'Career Force'? Implications for Ideology in the All-Volunteer Force." In *The Social Psychology of Military Service,* edited by Nancy L. Goldman and David R. Segal. Beverly Hills: Sage Publications, 1976. A shortened version appeared in *Armed Forces and Society* 2 (1975): 81–96.
Bachman, Jerald G., and Jennings, M. Kent. "The Impact of Vietnam on Trust in the Government." *Journal of Social Issues* 31 (1975): 141–56.
Badillo, Gilbert, and Curry, David G. "The Social Incidence of Vietnam Casualties." *Armed Forces and Society* 2 (1976): 397–406.

---

*Available from National Technical Information Service (NTIS), U.S. Dept. of Commerce, Springfield, VA 22161.

Bendix, Reinhard. *Nation-Building and Citizenship.* New York: John Wiley and Sons, Inc., 1964.

Bengtsson, Eva-Stina. "Some Political Perspectives of Academic Reserve Officers." *Journal of Peace Research* 3 (1968): 293–305.

Biderman, Albert D. "What is Military?" In *The Draft: A Handbook of Facts and Alternatives,* edited by Sol Tax. Chicago: University of Chicago Press, 1967.

Binkin, Martin, and Johnston, John D. *All-Volunteer Armed Forces: Progress, Problems, and Prospects.* Report prepared for the Committee on Armed Services, United States Senate, Ninety-Third Congress, First Session. Washington: U.S. Government Printing Office, 1973.

Blair, John D. "Civil-Military Belief Systems: Attitudes Toward the Military Among Military Men and Civilians." Ph.D. dissertation, University of Michigan, 1975.

———. "Emerging Youth Attitudes and the Military." In *The Changing American Military Profession,* edited by Franklin D. Margiotta. Boulder: Westview Press, 1977.

Blair, John D., and Bachman, Jerald G. "The Public View of the Military." In *The Social Psychology of Military Service,* edited by Nancy L. Goldman and David R. Segal. Beverly Hills: Sage Publications, 1976.

Blau, Peter M. *The Dynamics of Bureaucracy.* Chicago: University of Chicago Press, 1955.

Bowers, David G. "Navy Manpower: Values, Practices, and Human Resources Requirements." (Final report to the Office of Naval Research.) Ann Arbor: Institute for Social Research, 1975. (NTIS no. AD A014 493.)*

Bowers, David G., and Bachman, Jerald G. "Military Manpower and Modern Values." (Technical report to the Office of Naval Research, contract no. N00014–67–A–0181–0048, NR 170–746.) Ann Arbor: Institute for Social Research, 1974. (NTIS no. AD 787 826.)*

Browning, Harley L.; Lopreato, Sally C.; and Poston, Dudley L., Jr. "Income and Veteran Status." *American Sociological Review* 38 (1973): 74–85.

Campbell, Donald T., and McCormack, Thelma H. "Military Experience and Attitudes Toward Authority." *American Journal of Sociology* 62 (1957): 482–90.

Christie, R. "Changes in Authoritariansim as Related to Situational Factors." *American Psychology* 7 (1952): 307–8.

Coates, Charles H., and Pellegrin, Roland J. *Military Sociology.* University Park: The Social Science Press, 1965.

Converse, Phillip E. "The Nature of Belief Systems in Mass Publics." In *Ideology and Discontent,* edited by David E. Apter. New York: Free Press, 1964.

Cortright, David. *Soldiers in Revolt.* New York: Doubleday, 1975.

Cutright, Phillips. "The Civilian Earnings of White and Black Draftees and Non-Veterans." *American Sociological Review* 39 (1974): 317–27.

Davis, James W., Jr., and Dolbeare, Kenneth M. *Little Groups of Neighbors: The Selective Service System.* Chicago: Markham Publishing Company, 1968.

Davis, Vincent. "Levee En Masse, C'est Fini: The Deterioration of Popular Willingness to Serve." In *New Civil-Military Relations,* edited by John P. Lovell and Philip S. Kronenberg. New York: E. P. Dutton and Co., 1974.

Department of the Army. *Strength of the Army (U) Part II: Gains and Losses to Active Army.* Washington, May, 1975.

Domhoff, G. William. *Who Rules America?* Englewood Cliffs, New Jersey: Prentice-Hall, 1967.

Fligstein, Neil D. "Who Served in the Military? (1940–1973)." Paper presented at the meetings of the American Sociological Association. New York, 1976.

Franklin, Jerome L., and Drexler, John A. "Influences of Organizational Conditions and Practices on Reenlistment, Operational Readiness, and Satisfaction in the Navy." (Technical report to the Navy Personnel Research and Development Center.) Ann Arbor: Institute for Social Research, 1976.

French, Elizabeth G., and Ernest, Raymond R. "The Relationship Between Authoritarianism and the Acceptance of Military Ideology." *Journal of Personality* 24 (1955): 181–91.

Friedman, Milton. "Why Not a Volunteer Army?" In *The Draft: A Handbook of Facts and Alternatives,* edited by Sol Tax. Chicago: University of Chicago Press, 1967.

Goral, John "Major Findings from the May 1974 Gilbert Youth Survey of Attitudes Toward Military Service." Manpower Research and Data Analysis Center (MARDAC), report no. MR–75–2, 1975.

Goral, John, and Lipowitz, Andrea. "Attitudes of Youth Toward Military Service in the All-Volunteer Force." Manpower Research and Data Analysis Center (MARDAC), report no. MR–75–1, 1975.

Grusky, Oscar. "The Effects of Succession: A Comparative Study of Military and Business Organization." In *The New Military: Changing Patterns of Organization,* edited by Morris Janowitz. New York: Russell Sage Foundation, 1964.

Hauser, William L. *America's Army in Crisis: A Study in Civil-Military Relations.* Baltimore: John Hopkins University Press, 1973.

Helmer, John. *Bringing the War Home: The American Soldier in Vietnam and After.* New York: Free Press, 1974.

Huntington, Samuel P. *The Soldier and the State.* Cambridge: Harvard University Press, 1957. Reprint. New York: Vintage Press, 1964.

———. "Power, Expertise and the Military Profession." *Daedalus* 92: 785–807.

Inglehart, Ronald. "Changing Values and Attitudes Toward Military Service Among the American Public." In *The Social Psychology of Mili-*

tary Service, edited by Nancy L. Goldman and David R. Segal. Beverly Hills: Sage Publications, 1976.

Janowitz, Morris. *The Professional Soldier.* New York: Free Press, 1960.

———. "The Emergent Military." In *Public Opinion and the Military Establishment,* edited by Charles C. Moskos, Jr. Beverly Hills: Sage Publications, 1971.

———. "The U.S. Forces and the Zero Draft." *Adelphi Papers* 94 (1973): 1–30.

———. *Military Conflict.* Beverly Hills: Sage Publications, 1975.

Janowitz, Morris, and Moskos, Charles C., Jr. "Racial Composition in the All-Volunteer Force: Policy Alternatives." *Armed Forces and Society* 1 (1974): 109–23.

Jennings, M. Kent, and Markus, G. B. "The Effects of Military Service on Political Attitudes: A Panel Study." Paper presented at the Annual Meeting of the American Political Science Association. Chicago, Illinois, 1974.

Johnston, Jerome, and Bachman, Jerald G. *Youth in Transition, Volume V: Young Men and Military Service.* Ann Arbor: Institute for Social Research, 1972.

Karsten, Peter. " 'Professional' and 'Citizen' Officers: A Comparison of Academy and ROTC Officer Candidates." In *Public Opinion and the Military Establishment,* edited by Charles C. Moskos, Jr. Beverly Hills: Sage Publications, 1971.

Katz, Daniel; Gutek, Barbara A.; Kahn, Robert L.; and Barton, Eugenia. *Bureaucratic Encounters: A Pilot Study in the Evaluation of Government Services.* Ann Arbor: Institute for Social Research, 1975.

Keller, Suzanne. *Beyond the Ruling Class.* New York: Random House, 1963.

Kelman, H. C., and Lawrence, L. H. "Assignment of Responsibility in the Case of Lt. Calley." *Journal of Social Issues* 28 (1972): 177–212.

Kolko, Gabriel. *The Roots of American Foreign Policy.* Boston: Beacon Press, 1969.

Kronenberg, Philip S. "The Greening of the Brass: Emerging Civil-Military Relations." In *New Civil-Military Relations,* edited by John P. Lovell and Philip S. Kronenberg. New Brunswick: Transaction Books, 1974.

Lang, Kurt. "Technology and Career Management in the Military Establishment." In *The New Military: Changing Patterns of Organization,* edited by Morris Janowitz. New York: Russell Sage Foundation, 1964.

Larson, Arthur D. "Military Professionalism and Civil Control: A Comparative Analysis of Two Interpretations." *Journal of Political and Military Sociology* 2 (1974): 57–72.

Lasswell, Harold D. "The Garrison State." *American Journal of Sociology* 46 (1941): 455–68.

Lipset, Seymour Martin. "The Wavering Polls." *The Public Interest* 43 (1976): 70–89.

Lopreato, Sally Cook, and Poston, Dudley L., Jr. "Differences in Earnings and Earning Ability Between Black Veterans and Non-Veterans in the United States." Paper. Austin: University of Texas, 1976.

Lovell, John P. "The Professional Socialization of the West Point Cadet." In *The New Military: Changing Patterns of Organization,* edited by Morris Janowitz. New York: Russell Sage Foundation, 1964.

Lucas, William. "Anticipatory Socialization and the ROTC." In *Public Opinion and The Military Establishment,* edited by Charles C. Moskos, Jr. Beverly Hills: Sage Publications, 1971.

Marmion, Harry A. *The Case Against a Volunteer Army.* Chicago: Quadrangle Books, 1971.

Mason, William M. "On the Socio-Economic Effects of Military Service." Ph.D. dissertation, University of Chicago, 1970.

McClosky, Herbert. "Conservatism and Personality." *American Political Science Review* 52 (1958): 27–45.

Michaelsen, L. K. "A Methodology for the Studies of the Impact of Organizational Values, Preferences, and Practices in the All-Volunteer Navy." Ann Arbor: Institute for Social Research, 1973. (NTIS no. AD 763 769.)*

Miller, Arthur H. "Political Issues and Trust in Government: 1964–1970." *American Political Science Review* 68 (1974): 951–72.

Miller, J. C., and Tollison, R. "The Implicit Tax on Relevant Military Recruits." *Social Science Quarterly* 51 (1971): 924–31.

Mills, C. Wright. *The Power Elite.* New York: Oxford University Press, 1956.

Modigliani, Andre. "Hawks and Doves, Isolationism and Political Distrust: An Analysis of Public Opinion on Military Policy." *American Political Science Review* 66 (1972): 960–78.

Monsen, Joseph, Jr., and Cannon, Mark W. *The Makers of Public Policy: American Power Groups and Their Ideologies.* New York: McGraw-Hill, 1965.

Moskos, Charles C., Jr. *The American Enlisted Man.* New York: Russell Sage Foundation, 1970.

———. "The Emergent Military: Civil, Traditional, or Plural." *Pacific Sociological Review* 16 (1973a): 255–80.

———. "Studies on the American Soldier: Continuities and Discontinuities in Social Research." Paper presented at the Annual Meeting of the American Sociological Association. New York, 1973b.

———. "Social Control of the Military." Paper presented at the Annual Meeting of the American Sociological Association. San Francisco, 1975.

———. "Trends in Military Social Organization." Paper presented at the Conference on "The Consequences and Limits of Military Intervention." Chicago, 1976.

Mueller, John E. "Trends in Popular Support for the Wars in Korea and Vietnam." *American Political Science Review* 65 (1971): 358–75.

Oi, Walter Y. "The Costs and Implications of an All-Volunteer Force." In

The Draft: A Handbook of Facts and Alternatives, edited by Sol Tax. Chicago: University of Chicago Press, 1967.

Opinion Research Corporation. *Attitudes and Motivations Toward Enlistment in the U.S. Army.* Conducted for N. W. Ayer and Sons, Inc., and the U.S. Army. Princeton, New Jersey: Opinion Research Corporation, 1974.

Perrucci, Robert, and Pilisuk, Mark. "The Warfare State." In *The Triple Revolution Emerging*, edited by Robert Perrucci and Mark Pilisuk. Boston: Little, Brown and Company, 1971.

Robinson, John P., and Hefner, Robert. "Perceptual Maps of the World." *Public Opinion Quarterly* 32 (1968): 273–80.

Rodgers, Willard L., and Johnston, Lloyd D. "Attitudes Toward Business and Other American Institutions." Paper presented at the Annual Conference of American Association for Public Opinion Research, 1974.

Roghmann, Klaus, and Sodeur, Wolfgang. "The Impact of Military Service on Authoritarian Attitudes: Evidence from West Germany." *American Journal of Sociology* 78 (1972): 418–33.

Russett, Bruce M. "Political Perspectives of U.S. Military and Business Elites." *Armed Forces and Society* 1 (1974): 79–108.

Schuman, Howard. "Two Sources of Antiwar Sentiment in America." *American Journal of Sociology* 78 (1972): 513–37.

Segal, David R. "Civil-Military Relations in the Mass Public." *Armed Forces and Society* 1 (1975): 215–29.

———. " 'Worker Democracy' in Military Organization." In *The Changing American Military Profession*, edited by Franklin D. Margiotta. Boulder: Westview Press, 1977.

Segal, David R.; Blair, John; Newport, Frank; and Stephens, Susan. "Convergence, Isomorphism, and Interdependence at the Civil-Military Interface." *Journal of Political and Military Sociology* 2 (1974): 157–72.

Segal, David R., and Daina, Bernard L. *The Social Representativeness of the Volunteer Army.* Arlington: U.S. Army Research Institute for the Behavioral and Social Sciences Research Memorandum 75–12, 1975.

Segal, David R., and Segal, Mady W. "Models of Civil-Military Relationships at the Elite Level." In *The Perceived Role of the Military*, edited by M. R. Van Gils. Rotterdam: Rotterdam University Press, 1971.

———. "The Impact of Military Service on Trust in Government, International Attitudes, and Social Status." In *The Social Psychology of Military Service*, edited by Nancy L. Goldman and David R. Segal. Beverly Hills: Sage Publications, 1976.

Shils, Edward A., and Janowitz, Morris. "Cohesion and Disintegration in the Wehrmacht in World War II." *Public Opinion Quarterly* 12 (1948): 280–315.

Sjaastad, L. A., and Hansen, R. W. "The Conscription Tax: An Empirical Analysis." In *Studies Prepared for the President's Commission on an*

All-Volunteer Armed Force, Vol. II. Washington: U.S. Government Printing Office, 1970.

Spencer, Gregory. "A Methodology for the Studies of the Impact of Organizational Values, Preferences, and Practices on the United States Army." Ann Arbor: Institute for Social Research, 1975.

Stouffer, Samuel A. et al. *The American Soldier, Volume I: Adjustment to Army Life. Volume II: Combat and Its Aftermath.* Princeton, New Jersey: Princeton University Press, 1949.

Tax, Sol, ed. *The Draft: A Handbook of Facts and Alternatives.* Chicago: University of Chicago Press, 1967.

Times (London). September 17, 1974, p. 3.

U.S. President's Commission on an All-Volunteer Armed Force. *The Report of the President's Commission on an All-Volunteer Armed Force.* Washington: U.S. Government Printing Office, 1970.

Vagts, Alfred. *A History of Militarism.* New York: W. W. Norton, 1937.

Van Doorn, Jacques. *The Soldier and Social Change.* Beverly Hills: Sage Publications, 1975.

———. "The Military and the Crisis of Legitimacy." In *The Military and the Problem of Legitimacy,* edited by Gwyn Harries-Jenkins and Jacques Van Doorn. Beverly Hills: Sage Publications, 1976.

Yarmolinsky, Adam. "The American Military Role and Responsibility." *Naval War College Review* 27 (1974): 17–24.

Index